Cafe Abyss
John O'Brien's Fiction: A Reflection

edited by
Rob Jackson and David Megenhardt

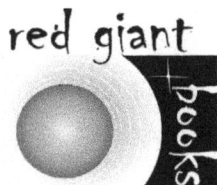

red giant
books

Cafe Abyss   John O'Brien's Fiction: A Reflection

Red Giant Books

ISBN: 978-1-7325514-2-8

10 9 8 7 6 5 4 3 2 1

Printed in the United States of America.

www.redgiantbooks.com

Contributors:

Sara Dobie Bauer, Christie Danzey, Dorian D'Apice, Kelly Flamos, Carolyn Jack, Cassandra Jackson, Alok Khorana, Matt Marshall, Ben Mckelvey, Max McNeil, Melissa Nahra, Tanya Pilumeli, Anna Powaski, Rick Ridgeway, Patrick Snee, Bob Triozzi, Erin O'Brien, Marina Vladova, and RA Washington
Carri Jackson: Proofreading
Samantha Jackson: Transcription
Natalie Grace Sipula: Copy Editor
Anna Powaski: Artwork
Front cover photo credit: Susan Rust
Back cover photo credit: Tim Lachina

A special thanks to Matt Marshall and Erin O'Brien for consulting and support. Thanks to Akashic for permission to reprint "The Tik" first published in *Las Vegas Noir*.

To Judith O'Brien

Enjoy your flight, and stop by your Our Abyss Café for a bite when you get sick of Club Average. It's the last turn before the terminal.

John O'Brien
Leaving Las Vegas

But let us leave him in the midst of that desert which he created for himself

Henry Miller
*The Time of the Assass*ins

Cafe Abyss
John O'Brien's Fiction
A Reflection

Introduction

Rob Jackson

The image of a writer as a drunken genius, tortured soul, isolated and misunderstood is nearly ubiquitous to the point of cliché. To think of a writer as conflicted and bridled with the disease of alcoholism brings to mind Malcolm Lowry (a writer who is mentioned several times independently by many contributors on the following pages), Charles Bukowski, Richard Yates, and Fredrick Exley, just to name a few. In many examples, it is only the alcohol that ties these various writers together. Lowry and Bukowski are as different writers as Gunter Grass is to Toni Morrison or as Alice Munro is to Roberto Bolano. The same goes for the works of John O'Brien. *Leaving Las Vegas* has very little in common with Bukowski's *Post Office* or Raymond Carver's *Where I'm Calling From*. There is very little material in, just to provide an additional example, *The Assault on Tony's* that would overlap with *Big Sur*. Great writers, even good writers, have more differences than similarities. However, the darkened spaces that would overlap in their Venn Diagram though small in area, like the nucleus of an atom, contain most of the mass.

Alcoholism works as a tragic flaw on the surface no different than greed, pride, gluttony, sex addiction or any of the drug addictions that individuals have struggled with from the hashish use in Charles Baudelaire's *Artificial Paradise* to the meth addicts explored in the work of Daniel Woodrell. These works aren't worthy because of the addictions; they are worthy because they are great works of literature. Another critical difference is that the writing of O'Brien has not yet reached the audience that the other writers mentioned have and, more than likely, never will. This fact, not only hasn't deterred any contributors in this book, from what I can tell, it has been more of an incentive than a deterrence. If *Leaving Las Vegas* had been sufficiently discussed, or widely enough read, I think we would have had few takers with this project.

After becoming intrigued, partly because of the challenge of writing about an unknown writer, who once resided in the greater Cleveland area, before considering joining in this project, the fundamental question went something like this: *what is it*? The only writers who agreed from the first to participate were Carolyn Jack (though even Carolyn had a caveat, she had reviewed one of John's books for *The Plain Dealer* a couple of decades before, and she wanted to reread it to make sure her opinion hadn't changed) and Rick Ridgway who didn't say yes or no but started musing about themes, sections, even quotes from *Leaving Las Vegas* in extraordinary detail, with an almost photographic memory, something he can do with hundreds of books and films. Watching his expression, though, transform from excitement to sadness, I realized this book had affected him deeply, and he would need some time to think this all through. He lowered his head and went silent. I knew this was a yes. He was in. Unfortunately, someone who could write so well once can no longer write because of illness. We would have to figure out a way to capture all of those unique thoughts about O'Brien one way or the other. I wish we could have gotten more, but the book is much better for the part we were able to include.

Others who had agreed to take part in this study, this *reflection*, which after rejecting "study," "critique," "appreciation," and "consideration," by process of elimination all that was left was *reflection*. Still, the adjective doesn't feel totally like it is the right word, but there was nothing left, and the word remains in the title because there were no other terms tossed about that came remotely close to what we were trying to do. I'll expand this term "reflection" when I return to the inspiration of Henry Miller's work.

I recently traveled to Las Vegas and read *Leaving Las Vegas* once again while I was there. Although about three decades have passed since O'Brien tells the story of Sera and Ben very little has changed about the city. The most significant difference is when people in the casinos are staring into a slot machine or at a poker table they are now staring into their smartphones, too. Other than that, O'Brien's details are striking. I even visited a 7-11, which may have been the very one that O'Brien mentions at the beginning of *Leaving Las Vegas*.

Sadly, because of his early, tragic death, the O'Brien catalog isn't extensive. The essays in this book will cover his novels *Better*, *Leaving Las Vegas*, *Stripper lessons* and *The Assault on Tony's* and the short story "The Tik," but only briefly in the afterword. We've decided to appendix "The Tik" with permission from Akashic Books, published in 2008 in *Las Vegas Noir* because if someone is so inclined to read all of John's prose, the piece would be the only work solely of O'Brien's which couldn't be easily found or tracked down. O'Brien's novel *Better*, the last book published chronologically also by Akashic Press, in 2009, *Stripper Lessons* and *The Assault on Tony's* were published by Grove Press in 1996 and 1997, respectively and *Leaving Las Vegas* was initially published by Watermark Press in 1991.

Why a book on John O'Brien? This idea had its genesis when I was talking to John's mother, Judith O'Brien, after a reading by Erin O'Brien when she released her book *The Irish Hungarian Guide to The Domestic Arts* at a gallery located in Lakewood, Ohio (John's hometown). It was a brief conversation with Judith, I told her *Leaving Las Vegas* is a book that had a tremendous impact on me, and I spent several minutes explaining why. Judith, or as I called her then, the only time I've met her up to the time of this writing, Mrs.O'Brien, was so appreciative that I took the time to speak with her about this but I wasn't quite sure if she thought I was just nice or if she understood the weight, the gravity, the impact that this novel could have in the hands of the right reader.

I felt then, maybe I should collect all of those improvised, scrambled thoughts that I shared with John and Erin's mother, and try to organize them and then express those ideas into an essay or perhaps even write a book. That night, in 2014, I sent an email to Dave Megenhardt, and told him what I felt we needed to do, and unlike most people, instead of saying "why", or "are you crazy", or something similar, because of the various projects that were already in process, including writing our own books, publishing other authors, and working with *Great Lakes Review*, he instead emailed something back along the lines of "I'm in, let's do it."

* * *

The mental template for me when thinking about a blueprint for this project has always been Henry Miller's *The Time of The Assassin*. As far as structures, if I want to talk about homecoming themes, from *Hamlet* to Pinter's *The Homecoming*, there is also the template of Homer's *The Odyssey*. If there's a treatise of one writer discussing another, where a reader learns some, as much, or more about the writer as the subject, I can think of none which accomplishes this to the degree of *The Time of the Assassins*. I'm going to expand this explanation more than once throughout this introduction and call upon Miller and Miller's subject as an influence and to some degree, a prototype. Miller's subject is the eccentric French 19th Century poet Arthur Rimbaud. This may seem like a detour, and maybe it is, but it won't be the last Henry Miller detour we will take.

Miller's "study," a term that he or a manager or a publisher or someone in between labeled it isn't a "study." This misnomer doesn't do the subtitle of his book justice. The title should not have been: *The Time of the Assassins a Study of Rimbaud by Henry Miller*. *The Time of the Assassins* is more of a therapy session for Miller than a study of Rimbaud for the world. Yes, It's much closer to a, you guessed it,

4

"reflection." It's not that we don't learn much about Rimbaud's work, we do. It's not that Miller does not become studious or academic at times. He does. This is just a slice of the book, though, and we also gain the opportunity to observe Miller's relationship with Rimbaud's work. Sometimes Miller disappears from the conversation and produces pages about his subject which could have been written by many people, but he always comes back. He is at times as much of a subject as Rimbaud. Once I decided to move forward with this book on John O'Brien of greater Cleveland, Ohio, I realized that Dave and I, and the small, dedicated group who believed in this project, should not solely critique, study, appreciate, or even, the runner up, create a *consideration*. I mentioned this approach to every contributor without mentioning the model being Miller's work. I didn't want anyone to run out or go online and order the book because observing the project through that lens may have changed or influenced the finished product. In fact, contributors will be learning this as they read this introduction for the first time.

Another reason I'm pleased that reflection was ultimately chosen over consideration, or for that matter, any other subtitle is that as the work came in, many of the pieces fit into that preferred subtitle. A few that did not still found styles and methods that analyze O'Brien's work lending insights far beyond comparatively if this project would have had a sole author. The writers who preferred keeping a distance, and examined the work with less subjectivity, keeping their personalities hidden to an extent, in the end, worked well balancing the project as a whole with the different styles chosen by writers who made themselves, their personalities and their direct experiences, part of the narrative. Furthermore, the pieces aren't all one way or the other, many fall all along the spectrum, expanding the possible views and voices, strengthening the whole.

Some would be labeled academic, others personal, a few even confessional to a degree, one would also be described more as a review or perhaps an article. We gave writers few boundaries, especially as they worked on their original ideas. We tried to make it clear that there were really no wrong answers and we encouraged taking risks. If something doesn't seem to be working, let's discuss, brainstorm, mark the piece up, go where thoughts may take you, we encouraged, making assurances that we can mold the piece later.

Reading John O'Brien's work, wasn't on many, well come to think of it any of the contributors' reading list. They read his work because I suggested they do so because of something I had read by them, sometimes a poem, a part of a memoir, or a piece of fiction either at a reading or in print, something they brought forth about their own life and work, compelled me to approach them with this project. Out of the several dozens of creative people who I have seen read at an event or whose work I have come across in print in the last decade or so, I felt that these individuals should join us in this reflection, and with just an exception of a couple, who were buried in the middle of their own work, all were interested and delivered work that added layers of meaningful discussion to this project. As I read through the essays and discussions, I came across so much insight that this introduction has been halved as I removed my own thoughts about the works when I found similar or even exact views expressed by contributors.

* * *

Another method that transformed what a book like this could be is a book club that Dave invited me to be a part of after the original idea of making this book a reality in 2014. I came to realize that some of the most erudite, worldly, discerning readers that I know weren't all writers: they were also physicians, judges, attorneys, photographers, visual artists, architects and, coincidentally, an owner of a bar. Susan DeGaetano from Mac's Backs in Coventry recommended a bar proprietor who happened to be an avid reader and, her bar, coincidentally, is located in John's hometown. The fact that one of John's books takes place in a bar and one of the contributors for *The Assault on Tony's* is a bar owner and a bibliophile is a combination we couldn't have scripted, which brought yet one more unique perspective.

There are no discussions in Miller's book on Rimbaud, and there aren't even other voices. I don't believe there is a book written about a writer that includes what Dave and I have decided to do with this book. We have discussions, roundtables, that are transcribed with impromptu thoughts, and these improvisations create insight that an essayist alone may not capture, though the comparison is unjust because the writers in this book reach places that interruptions from a roundtable would have stunted at best and annihilated at worst. By including some of the most articulate readers we know, though they are outside of traditional fields when one thinks of books or literary endeavors, my understanding of O'Brien's works have been expanded, and I am appreciative of that fact. Because of the nature of roundtables, we have edited for brevity and clarity while keeping intent.

Once we made up our minds to go in this direction, we included diverse voices. College students, for example, not that far away in age from when O'Brien wrote some of his earlier work. The novel *Better* has younger characters, some who may have just dropped out of college, congregating at a place where troubled or confused college-age adults of today may find a situation in which to disappear. Notably, young people could be influenced under the magnetism of Double Felix, a character with sides of fictional characters and historical persons, from Jay Gatsby to Howard Hughes, a bit before the time of one of the more eccentric, wealthy entrepreneurs of today's tech world. If we are going to have a reflection of John O'Brien's work, then let's include younger people, mainly if the goal of this book maintains, no matter how limited, that John O'Brien's books will be read years from now. If we are going to talk about *Stripper Lessons*, let's have a roundtable with only women. *The Assault on Tony's* is the book O'Brien, I believe, had race and politics on his mind, so it was essential to have diverse views when discussing all the implications of his last, unfinished work.

This is a good place to discuss unfinished and finished work. There is some debate about what constitutes finished and unfinished during some of these conversations and some ruminating in the essays too. Here is my uncertain view: *Leaving Las Vegas* and his short story "The Tik" are the only two works discussed that I consider finished. With that stated, there are many with very well-thought out arguments which differ. *The Assault on Tony's* was beyond doubt unfinished, and this is well documented. I consider *Stripper Lessons* to be unfinished, but I do think it is a complete draft. For me to consider a work finished, the manuscript would have to be edited with proof of revisions. There are clues that an editor, either professional or otherwise, did not work with John on what I think was a draft. Now, the fact that it was a draft does not mean that he wasn't ready to submit the work for publication, or an agent, it merely means that especially pre-internet/email it would have made no sense to do substantial revisions beyond the first couple of chapters. In the late '80s and the early '90s, the first couple of chapters along with a summary, perhaps chapter synopsis, a small summary, or some combination of these choices would still have been normally all the further a writer would have progressed before an agent or a publisher then asked for more chapters or the remainder of the manuscript. Before getting to this point, what sense would it make to work on sentence structures, awkward transitions, mistakes of time, and place, for instance? Especially since the submission would have been made by snail mail and could have easily taken up to a year to hear any response.

This is why it is hard to criticize if the theory is correct, errors such as sequence, point of view, or a myriad of other issues that working with an editor through a revision process would have easily fixed. When there are sentence structures or awkward transitions that do not seem to fit with a writer who has sometimes dozens of pages without such issues, one can easily imagine those issues were things that can be fixed later...just place the words on the page first, craft later. It's important to note, working with an editor on revisions, obviously, is not the same as proofreading or copy editing. I have no doubt these things were done to one degree or the other, but those errors (typos basically) would simply be distractions, not a change in character or story. The novel *Better*, for example, is clean but if John knew that it would be published would he have taken another look at it? This is not a new discussion. Milan Kundera wrote an intriguing book *Testaments Betrayed*, where he discusses in length the ramifications of publishing posthumous work, finished and unfinished. I recommend it for a fuller discussion on this topic. After reading Kundera and others and thinking this subject though, I've come to the conclusion that this is way too complex for a binary choice, and there isn't necessarily a universal correct answer.

The most famous example of this is probably the case of Franz Kafka and Max Brod. With a terminal tuberculosis diagnosis, Kafka instructed his friend and agent to destroy the work which he had earlier sent to him. If Brod had honored his client's wishes, we wouldn't have three modern masterpieces: *The Trial*, *The Castle*, and *Amerika*, not to mention essential stories. At the very minimum, *Amerika* is just one example of a draft, characters are introduced with no real development and then disappear, there are other things that do not add up, and this doesn't seem to be Modernism or Absurdism, nor does it appear to be the eponymous Kafkaesque. If Kafka would have had more time, many scholars believe that draft would have been revised into a completed, polished novel. Two points to make here: 1. Since a final draft wasn't published, is it a meaningful criticism to point out draft-like qualities? 2. Can posthumous, published drafts have literary merit? I would argue no on the first point and yes on the second. *Amerika*, an amazing book, proves the second point beyond a doubt, along with dozens of other works discussed elsewhere, including the work of writers such as Robert Musil and Nikolia Gogol (who actually burned the second part of *Dead Souls*).

As a reader, I'm searching for literary merit in a finished, much-revised work or a fragmentary work that marks the beginning of an experience that I mentally or physically will respond to, hopefully both. However, to find or to judge the merits of the latter, I have to use a different scale. I've made the analogy of a chef who has to judge a recipe before the dish is fully cooked, sometimes by just looking at the recipe. A skilled chef can do this, but she or he would have to bring experience to be able to appreciate the potential of how the dish would have tasted? It's far from a perfect analogy, but I'm unsure if there is a better one.

This is why I have felt it necessary to go into such depth about this point. The easiest book John O'Brien wrote for someone to discuss or write about is *Leaving Las Vegas*, from there it becomes more challenging from *Better* to *Stripper Lessons*, leading to the most challenging work to discuss because obviously, it is the least completed of his posthumous works, *The Assault on Tony's*. For the participants who either discussed *Leaving Las Vegas* or wrote about that particular novel, had one less duty, one less thought to cross the mind, no what-ifs, wondering if this or that part would have been changed or developed more or this scene cut and on and on.

Ultimately, if any of John's books are read in fifty years, which would be a substantial accomplishment, an accomplishment that any writer would sign up for if that was the choice before any career was started, no matter how successful that career became later on, that book would with little doubt be *Leaving Las Vegas*. If this effort does nothing else, but in some small way, helps propel this potential American classic into its right place and helps readers continually discover it, then no matter how little that effect may be, this work will exceed any expectations for any involved who helped make it a reality. If this book encourages any readers to go beyond *Leaving Las Vegas*, which I hope it does, then we are in positive territory. While *Leaving Las Vegas* is complete, accomplished, devastating, unique followed by many other adjectives that I could easily add, to witness John as an artist by experiencing his other works can bring great satisfaction, too.

By praising *Leaving Las Vegas*, my intent is not to diminish his other writing but only to call attention to the fact that this work can and should be judged on another level. Finished, revised, mature, publishing intent, and the rest. Every word John O'Brien would write would occur before he turned thirty-four years old, and through some of the discussions in this book many will ponder what could have been if the exceptional talent he showed, again, particularly in *Leaving Las Vegas*, a novel started when he was only in his twenties, may have matured further and his fiction may have reached even greater heights. Is that question futile? I lean toward no and this is one of the reasons this book is an exploration of all his novels.

There was some discussion between Dave and me about making this a three-person team as far as editing, direction, or any other of the multitude of choices about the approach or formation of this book by merely inviting Erin O'Brien whom we have both known for years. The choices we made for the creation of this book were wide-ranging including choices such as who we invited to participate, what material we decided to add in the appendix, to what parts we ultimately chose not to include, and just about every other editorial choice one can imagine. After some discussion, we only asked Erin to be available for questions and to consult as needed. She graciously offered to assist us in any way she could. She shared with us information about the books, including the writing and the publications that only she would know, and that information, which we could have gotten nowhere else, was invaluable. We also asked her if we could share her contact information with other writers who may have questions that we did not have the answer to and, in true Erin fashion, she was always willing to do what she could, and that offer of assistance was crucial to the writers who called on her for certain facts or clarifications, including this one.

There were basically two reasons we decided to keep this a two-person editorial team. One simply was because we thought the contributors might feel more open and if any of them had something less than favorable to express or something that may be awkward in any sense, and there are some who do, then the writer or participant could be as open and honest as possible. When we invited Erin to one of the roundtables, we made the decision only to invite her to part two of the discussion, to help ensure the participants felt at ease to speak freely because the questions and format of part one.

This is not to say that opinions expressed freely wouldn't have happened anyway, but this way helped ensure as much. The first reason, though, pales in comparison to the second, and that is because Erin has done almost all the heavy lifting when it comes to her brother's legacy. We thought she should accept the opportunity to let someone else take over the driving, at least for a little while. Just, hopefully, enjoy the experience--the process-- with her proverbial feet up on the coffee table, hand the baton off and take a break without stopping the race. Continuing with the relay metaphor, we did ask her to consider taking the anchor by penning an afterward which after some consideration, she agreed to do and we couldn't be more satisfied with that decision and its result.

We nudged contributors, within reason, to reflect more on John's work than his life. We didn't make anything out of bounds, but when we felt an essay perhaps turning more into biography than concentrating on the work, we made suggestions and helped shape the piece back toward the art, not the artist. Part of the reason for this, and we didn't try to curb anyone's curiosity about John's life in relation to his works, is that we thought it would be appropriate for many of these questions to be answered by the best source in the afterword. Erin concludes this book (with the exception of the appendix) by answering many of the questions the contributors have throughout the book and brings this idea that was launched in 2014 to an eloquent and informational conclusion.

Now that I've just explained how we encouraged writers to talk more about the writing than the writer, I'm going to ignore our own encouragement. In fact, I'm just going to disregard this and discuss the writer to a point. To do this I must refer back to near the beginning regarding the influence, or better yet one of the inspirations for *Cafe Abyss*, Henry Miller's *Time of The Assassins*, that short book, treatise, "study" that bears little resemblance to *Cafe Abyss*, no more than O'Brien to Rimbaud but as I read Miller express "In Rimbaud's case the awakening was in death. The little light which flickered out with his demise grew in power and intensity as the fact of his death became more largely known. He has lived more wondrously and vividly than he ever did in life. One wonders, if he had come back *in this life*, what sort of poetry would he have written, what his message would have been. It was though, cut off in the prime of his manhood, he was cheated of that final phase of manhood which permits a man to harmonize his warring selves."

The five words "cheated of that final phase" can apply to so many circumstances and in my office located in my basement taking the baton from Henry Miller, I wonder too. Wonder about a parallel universe where bookshelves contain works written by writers during old age. The poems of a graying Percy Bysshe Shelley, Sylvia Plath, and John Keats. Plays by the octogenarians Lorraine Hansberry and Georg Buchner, novels by the aged John Kennedy Toole, Stephen

Crain and Emily Bronte.

Yes, these are all the well-known cases but if I had to guess how many John O'Brien types which are relatively unknown compared to these historic writers mentioned who have left this world with many possible unwritten or unfinished works the number would favor the latter by many factors. For the sake of this narrow point, John O'Brien could easily be swapped out by an equally, maybe lesser-known, maybe more-known, writer such as Breece D'J Pancake (1952-1979). The obscure Breece Pancake mirrors John O'Brien's situation more closely than the historical, legendary Shelley, Bronte, or Keats. With six stories published during his lifetime and six after, not to mention how he chose to end his life.

I'll wind this down, naturally, with more thoughts about Henry Miller. Not the historical Henry, but the fictional Henry that has just popped into existence. He's thinking about, daydreaming about, a parallel universe, unlike our own vacuous universe where Rimbaud and Van Gogh both left Las Vegas also in their '30s, both "cut off in the prime" each born and died one year apart, in this parallel universe the seventy-nine-year-old Rimbaud's writings continue well into the 20th Century, further immortalized by a painting created by the seventy-eight-year-old Vincent Van Gogh, and fifty years removed by their personal Seasons in Hell, living long enough to witness Europe's season in hell, the war to end all wars, and now they sit among the sunflowers in the south of France: the old men writing, painting; writing, painting, the two sages sharing a bottle of French wine, writing...painting. In this parallel France, Van Gogh's finishing a portrait of the old poet which will someday bring more money at an auction than either artist are equipped to conceive either by their history, their epoch, or their evolution.

My eyes remain closed, still, in the parallel universe, I come to the Os on a bookshelf. John O'Brien, four completed novels, revised, edited and then on to his novels written in his forties, 50s, and 60s, all lined up in a row, much like the novels of Philip Roth just a few letters away on this alphabetized bookshelf. The recovery stories? The triumphant victory over addiction? Perhaps a sequel where we learn what happens to Sera or Carroll (did he end up marrying Jennifer?) later in life. *Rehab to Redemption,* a study (reflection!) of the later works perhaps?

Reality intrudes, back to this universe. We have an early short story, some scripts, one finished, polished, edited novel which I have no problem proclaiming to be an American masterpiece and three other novels which were completed to various stages and, while incomplete, shows promise that John had a chance, a very good chance to develop into a great American novelist, joining a group few in number. Back to Roth again, skipping ahead three letters; if he would have died before the age of 34, we wouldn't even have the early novel *Portnoy's Complaint,* not to mention the nearly thirty novels after until his death at 85. Roth had decades to "harmonize his warring self." John O'Brien found no harmony in his self and lost the war, leaving space on our bookshelves eternally empty.

Leaving Las Vegas

An Introduction to Leaving Las Vegas
Rick Ridgeway

"The desert's quiet, Cleveland's cold, so the story ends, we're told."

-Townes Van Zandt

From the mind of John O'Brien, we are introduced to a legendary, morbid alcoholic who decides to end it all in Las Vegas, which seems like a logical decision, after becoming acquainted with the character Ben, even though he is beyond logic. Las Vegas, a city that extols glittery vulgarity, including an architecture that coaxes tourists into the illusion of possible, though highly improbable, wealth and power. What could be better? What could really have any equivalence with Las Vegas? Most places that can compare to the city's illusional and delusional power over people are mythical: El Dorado, Shangri-La, even semi-mythical places like Xanadu. Las Vegas is a semi-mythical place all in one, both illusion and reality. If it hadn't existed already, it could have been dreamt up by Donald Trump, boiled up out of his subconscious.

The novel's two main characters, Ben and Sera, have a fineness of soul that's elusive but always noticeable. Extraordinarily, they need both their nakedness and their privacy, especially Sera. Sera suffers horribly and accepts it all. It's a form, though slight, of masochism, which inevitably leaves the reader with an unsettling feeling long after the last word of the novel. Just to note a few of these painful experiences: teenagers gang rape her; a slob urinates on her; and a vengeful pimp abrades her. Yet, O'Brien always hovers - never sentimentally - as he patiently creates the character of Sera, eventually bridging her story to Ben's, who doesn't appear until the book is a fourth of the way over; and only then does O'Brien begin to reveal one of the main themes of the novel: that friendship and kindness are the elixirs to the cruelty of this world.

However, I'm getting ahead of myself - I have more to say about Sera. In the throes of striving in her battle to save Ben, Sera is revealed as a true heroine. She is not some cliché "good" prostitute. Instead, she's a woman portrayed as a multi-faceted human being who has a complex and contradictory personality. She has a core of goodness mixed with, among other impenetrable traits, a shocking acceptance of submission.

Ben is even more difficult to summarize. The few traces of explanation about his history suggest that he was a salesman at one time, perhaps successfully. I can testify from my own experience that this is a profession that can lead easily enough to overindulgence with alcohol due to its combination of stress and what many successful salesmen feel initially is a potential path to extraordinary success. We can only imagine what O'Brien went through before he wrote the novel, but it's insulting to him to consider it an autobiography. He must've had an underlying foundation to draw upon; reserves of knowledge, imagination, and sobriety. All the stuff of life. Yet, even with those reserves at his disposal, one still wonders where he got the guts to write it? And did those guts, paradoxically, kill him not long after it was written? I can't help but be curious about such questions, as so many others have been after reading the novel, but it is important that those curiosities don't cloud our understanding of the novel, because from the first word on page one to the last word concluding the novel, all that matters is Ben, Sera, and to a lesser extent Al and a handful of minor characters. The novel, to be fully appreciated, must be read and understood as just that - a work of imagination, not one of autobiography.

The book is courageous and very extreme, and by extreme, I mean it makes you watch in detail precisely what you don't want to watch. For some critics, who inexplicably gave it negative reviews, O'Brien went too far in this regard. For some reason, a few critics just couldn't stand the thought that people like Ben and Sera exist. I guess the thought of it must've ruined their mood for that evening's cocktail parties. I could name names and provide quotes and expose the shoddiness of a few, but I've somewhat mellowed in old age. Instead, I will simply say that when you hold a mirror up to reality, you might get more truth than you bargained for. This is true of many profound novels, including some of the greatest to have ever been written.

It's not just the experience of the alcoholic or the aspects of his life that O'Brien has mastered. This man could write. A good writer finds what he needs; a great writer finds everything. While there are so many masterful writing sections, and I wish I could share many more that I have underlined in my copy, I realize this is not feasible, but I want to share at least this one.

"The oppressive air hangs still above the street and seems to sweat the inexhaustible supply of perennial refuse that surrounds and infiltrates every scene. The filth of the road is blown on to the sidewalk, from there pushed against the buildings, finally coming to its semi-permanent resting place under ledges and in doorframes of abandoned businesses. Empty wine bottles wearing paper bags and newspaper circulars telling stories about produce and canned spaghetti served as the makings of a disposable bed for disposable humans. Doors that would pass for nailed shut open briefly and spit out black men wearing leather blazers and berets who stoop at the passenger window of a waiting Cadillac; A moment later the car pulls away. Bob's Lucky Stop Liquor No. 6 is shutting down for the night. A Korean man, presumably Bob, pulls along an iron track the first three black accordion security gates that, when closed, go nicely with similar iron that covers the display window. Painted on its glass, behind the bars is a smiling blond dressed in black velvet and holding a glass of whiskey: Ben's Dream: prisoner of a liquor store. So far there are no woman for hire, but then he's still too far east; perhaps closer to Western. He drives on."

Writing this rich exhibits not only mastery of the form, but also has an element of mystery to it that leaves the reader wondering how the author could conjure up such a scene out of mere words. When I read O'Brien, I am not simply reading words on a page, but instead find myself standing among the words as the author describes to me (directly to me, mind you, and no one else) what the character sees and the way it makes him feel. It is all very subtle; you'll find no heavy-handiness here; and if you can't feel it - if you need spoon fed to be immersed in the world of this scene - than perhaps O'Brien isn't the author for you.

My shelves are full of books from writers who struggled with alcohol and wrote about alcoholic characters. Some are well known, such as Faulkner, Hemingway, Fitzgerald, and Cheever; while others are lesser known, but equally as talented, such as Theodore Weesner. I've been asked what other books I would compare to *Leaving Las Vegas*. Honestly, I wouldn't know what book to compare it to. Has anybody ever conceived something so extreme and then delivered it with near perfection and then killed themselves? A combination of death pact and perfect aesthetic pact? What would it be? It's an inconceivable thing to do, and yet he did it.

I think it would be just about the hardest assignment a writer could give her or himself: write a story about a profoundly human character who has no hope, none. The fact that he is compassionate, intelligent, and sees meaning outside of his own situation makes the assignment seem that much more impossible. A duty to write it through to the very hellish end. Go ahead, try it...I dare you.

However, when pressed to come up with a book to which *Leaving Las Vegas* can be compared, I would choose Malcolm Lowry's *Under the Volcano*, because I believe the two novels share similar objectives.

Yet, in terms of barren hopelessness, Lowry's Geoffrey is still far away from the place Ben has entered. Geoffrey may have gotten there if he wouldn't have been murdered first.

Also, as a final point, I want to acknowledge another way in which this book is unique within the literary canon, which is found when one considers it as a love story. I'm going to make the bold claim that it is the most original love story ever written. By that, I simply mean that is isn't necessarily the best or the most transcendent love story, but that as far as love stories go, it is incomparable. I can think of compelling, haunting, sublime love stories throughout the history of literature, but for all of them I can think of others that influenced them, or ones which they influenced, or ones they just coincidentally share similarities with. However, that is not the case with *Leaving Las Vegas*. O'Brien's novel, as a love story, stands alone.

Leaving Las Vegas Roundtable
Part One

Erin O'Brien (Part Two)
Rob Jackson
Dave Megenhardt
Alok Khorana
Bob Triozzi
Ben McKelvey

Rob: Let's discuss John's age when he started the book. I was surprised when I first read the book because I didn't know that he was so young- only in his late 20s- and while it really didn't change any aspect of the book for me, it has often made me think of what he could have written with another twenty or thirty years of experience. And so I just want to get your thoughts on that so we'll start with you, Ben.

Ben: Right into the newbie. I'm happy to bat leadoff. I would say that right at the outset you can't help but notice that for someone in his 20s, and you realize he passed away when he was 33, and to have accumulated the level of experience that he possessed in order to write a book like this is staggering at the very least, insight into this gritty world of the rejected person, of the addicted person, and more specifically a really in-depth, almost psychological, playbook.

A play by play breakdown of how such a person goes about pursuing his addiction and we assume, from learning a little bit about his life, is probably somewhat based on firsthand experience but yet again to think about a person in their 20s, and he hits upon this a couple of times in the book, that he might have difficulty reaching for cash to

22

pay the bartender to the point where he needs to ask the bartender if he can grab his wallet for assistance and a number of other incidents where the bartender is not necessarily looking disapprovingly at him in the sense of wanting to kick him out, but just feeling a moral pull of "I can't believe I'm looking at a young person who's in this sort of state."

So yeah I thought it was really hard to wrap my head around the fact that he was so young and had lived so hard but it's a little bit of a cliché too. The brightest lights burn out fast, they burn hard, they die young. And I think he's an example of that. Someone who has found such a clear and beautiful literary voice and to have accumulated that level of experience is just kind of extraordinary. I had a difficult time relating to it and I'm 34 right now. So I'm one year older than he was when he died. I'm close enough to my 20s, and I appreciate literature, and then I read something like this, and I think about his life and I realize just how much separation there is.

So both in experience and the artistic capability it's hard to believe what age he was, those are a few thoughts I had concerning his age..

Dave: So I think the book, the character is viewed as a romantic, the book a tragic Romanticism. Right? So that's where his age comes out in the tone.

I have a hard time in how you pose the question to somebody who happens to be fifty and beyond. People in their 50s, if they have 30 years of this, do not have that sort of "I'm gonna die tragically, I'm gonna propel towards this end." They've lived the life of despair. You can't help but think of Bukowski or the writers of that are sort of alcoholic and who struggle with it throughout their lifetime. So, I think that there is that in it and I also think that the fact that you don't really know why too, why he's doing this ,speaks to his age. It doesn't appear to be a divorce. He was divorced, yes, but how long could he have been married? I mean to your point, the process is so sped up that when he talks about leaving a suicide note and it's a long suicide note, I'm kinda stumbling for the ideas because it's like they're all confused in my mind as far as how somebody that is this young comes to this point. But there is some part that is not desperate, that it's not the end, it doesn't feel like the end, it feels much more heroic when he's at the end of his rope and *that's* written by a young person.

Alok: So I was shocked when I realized he was in his late twenties when he wrote it. I had to go back and check and it was published when he was exactly 30 so that makes sense that he wrote it in his late 20s. Even though he ended his life, one doesn't want to conflate the author with the primary narrator.

There may be some overlap there, but there may not be. It can't clearly know coming to the book; we can guess. So in the book, I kept imagining him as being maybe in...I didn't watch the movie... in his 40s or 50s but not really in his 20s; he had a lot of maturities. I guess that speaks to the assumptions you make about young people who write well… readers think they are older if they don't have that information beforehand. Even with that in mind, with this particular book, it's still surprising. I mean we've read authors in their 20s and the literary sensibility is usually different. This is a very mature sensibility. Even though what he is doing is essentially committing a very prolonged suicide.

So you know I'm a cancer physician and I have a lot of young patients and usually the struggle is just grasping to get that extra time and here's somebody who's young and could have extra time and that, and we assume that he could stop if he wanted to...well we don't really know if he could stop the suicide at least that's my perception of this and, instead of stopping, he's just trying to accelerate it. It's really a loss.

Rather than trying to correct it, there's not even an attempt at trying to stop what's happening. Even when Sera sort of politely suggests to him there may be a way back, he becomes upset. He wants to end it in a certain way and that's it.

So I was really shocked by the age thing and I think that's something that would never be guessed if someone didn't tell you about the author. I would have never guessed it.

Dave: So let me follow up with that. So if you're shocked that he's giving in to addiction, does it work for somebody that young?

Alok:: As the narrator?

Dave: As in the book, Ben not John. So you know if the bartender is shocked that he's so young and it's so far outside of our experience to see somebody that young being this fatalistic. It's such a point in the book, right, that he's giving in to addiction this early.

Bob: I think for everybody to view it that way, it's depending on the person's makeup and how they respond physically to the addiction.

I have seen people age very quickly and you see people often times and you're stunned to learn how young they are, given how they present themselves and what they actually look like physically...not to mention what their belief system may be. The toll that addiction takes on people is severe, it's severe.

Alok: To some extent, it's more than an addiction- It's just this headlong rush into just wanting to die, that's not just pure addiction, there are other factors at play. Right? To my mind, sole addiction is like what's happening with the opioid crisis. Addiction isn't always coupled with the desire of not wanting to exist.

Bob: The part about not wanting to exist, you don't know. Here is what I mean: he's 30 and he's not a kid. And the fact that he seemed to of had a loving, stable marriage, my sense is that he went through a whole lot....between from whenever it was he started drinking excessively to this point--had tried very hard to change, to adjust himself so that he would preserve those things in his life that were important to him and we're seeing him at a point in his life despite when his efforts.... it's one failure after another.

We don't see that part in the book, what life events brought him to that point...I thought it was very moving when he is wearing his wedding ring again--that was clearly a part of his life that I think he longed for. If he could have, he wouldn't have behaved in a way that leads all the folks to pass judgment on him, if he could have acted differently, he would have, but we're picking up on his story well past the point of no return for him.

Rob: Before the book started, he decides that either he doesn't want to live or he can't live. At some point, he comes to the realization that this is something he can't kick. As bad as he may have wanted to prior to the reader being introduced to the character, he'll never be able to overcome this, or at least that decision has been made final before the first word in the book.

Bob: To your question about John, you know it was interesting, something in my mind sticks that Sera is 29.

Rob: Yes that's true.

Bob: So there's a part of this that, you know, is about characters and circumstances of himself that he must have known. When we talk about a writer, I've heard, because I'm not a writer, that writers are given advice to write about what they know. And clearly he, in reading this, I mean...he rang the bell...I mean I was very moved by this...it was remarkable how well he expressed all of that. I'm not sure he ever would have made it to 50 unless he addressed his addiction issues. And even if he had, what would that have looked like? What would he know? I don't think he could ever replicate this. We're at that age, some of our favorite rock stars and stuff, you know, it was back during the crazy days where they did their best material and it was hard for them and if that's what's moving you and inspiring you, as you get older, what happens when that dissipates? And what do you have to say now.

I'm not sure that I would look to him as somebody, as he was turning 50, who could have been at this level of wonderful writing and could have accomplished that level...I just don't know the answer to that, but he rang the bell with this, in my opinion.

Ben: I'd like to make a little observation, I'm glad that you brought up Sera and I think it's interesting that we start out with this reflection on John O'Brien the author and we immediately identified with Ben the character and we kind of overlooked Sera who is not only a key figure in the book but the author leads off with Sera.

I think that's an incredibly important and interesting fact about the book. But I also think it's interesting that people identified this narrative with alcoholism first when it also addresses a different pattern of self-destructive behavior.

Sera herself describes, in the language of addiction, she talks about her pattern being upset after that horrible rape incident in the beginning and how she has a very hard time coming to terms with the fact that she can't go back to what she knows and what she does well and how it controls her life—there's this control element of it, also just this notion that we, I use the big WE, not just us at this table. I think it's kind of natural for people to think about someone, like a young man in his 20s or a writer in his early 30s, writing about alcoholism at this level, this almost unimaginable level, at least for a lot of people. But we all skirt over the fact that this girl is portrayed as having immediately transitioned into prostitution and the implications of that experience.

Bob: If John hadn't killed himself, how would this discussion be informed? I mean because we sort of view this more as his story, but with Sera, I agree with you completely. Sera is as much a part of what he's trying to tell us. Maybe that's the tension in his life...he's probably, while he's writing this, I'm speaking off the cuff here...really that the fact that the contemplation of suicide may be happening at some point and has entered into his mind, at what point? With the information we have we have no way of knowing.

There's a point in the book where she can't understand suicide, she can't understand how anybody of this species could ever get to that point. For Ben it's almost like pick your path., Path A, the Sera path and trying to decide if this is the road to take and if that's the case how do you respond to that? or path B the one that Ben actually took. I mean this could well be that Sera and Ben are both John...or at least certainly at that point in the book they are both John; they are different sides of the same person.

Alok: I guess, though, just to come back to the age thing for a second, one of the things I thought about was to know this level of almost a depraved level of being alcoholic, and this description is so specific... you know...the shaking of the hands and these scenes where someone needs to put the dollar bills in his front pocket because sometimes he's so drunk that he can't reach into his wallet and take the bills out. So I know I said let's separate the narrator and the writer, but if you conflate them, then ok you can see yeah-- he has had this first-person experience, at some point he went through this in his 20s and then he managed to extricate himself a little bit to be able to finish this little masterpiece and then he relapsed? That's kind of a scary thought.

Rob: I think the book works entirely on its own, but your mind goes there and because you think if a real person experienced any of this, it's so harsh.

It's almost impossible not to have it enter your mind. A question: do you think it's unfair or misguided at all to bring in the life of the author when you're judging the book? Or any work of fiction? And let me preface by saying that's one thing about this book that Dave and I are trying to achieve, it's not a solely a literary study, I would categorize it more of an anthropological study which includes literature.

Any thoughts on that? Ben?

Ben: That's a really interesting question and I like the approach to what we're doing right now, this notion of a roundtable, it's not necessarily overly obsessed with literary formalism and more talking about the general human themes and acknowledging the life of the author. But no I think that's an important point, you can't fall asleep on that issue of who's the narrator and what is that perspective. But to answer your question yeah, I think that you have to pay attention to who John is and his life and to this point, this relentlessly specific guidebook to executing the alcoholic plan and it's so excruciating to read, so horrifying to read, and at one point he says something along the lines of not just possessed physically, but possessed mentally or spiritually or something along those lines. And I think that's something where if you have any exposure to people who suffered deeply from addiction, you know that it's a complete psychological possession. And that's really what comes through with all of this. And so I don't know how you disentangle someone who had the ability to execute that narrative from holy hell how does someone come into that level of knowledge. The same thing for Sera.

Bob: Concerning Sera, work was incredibly important to her, she had this level of confidence—that whole part about what she does, she has this high competence for living in this highly violent, dangerous world, and how she was able to manage this was almost the same thing, as far as navigating the difficulties. Two sides of the same coin concerning how they approached their lives.

They felt the need to be tightly managed with this high level of competence. The way Ben is doing it, it's brilliant. He understands the opening and closing time to all of the bars, how to read bartenders, how he's going to navigate through this world that's dangerous, but also not accepting it. Sera does the *exact* same thing. How she manages her life in the casino, how she manages her trick, all of that, is very well thought out and managed.

Dave: What was your reaction when Al comes on the scene and she falls right back into being his woman?

Bob: I had a lot of problems with that. I did... everything I've learned about her to that point...I was not comfortable with how she just fell right back into that. She had already broken loose. And the ease at which she, I mean, maybe that's just power, in a way when we talk about the power of addiction, for her it was the power of fear maybe?

Dave: Masochism possibly?

Rob: Stockholm Syndrome?

Bob: Completely crippled by that...didn't rest easy with me.

Dave: To the point that it changes her personality too. She's asking to be hit, asking to be abused, and you feel that when she's abused by the jocks, it felt more like a violation than where this is something like it's an established pattern.

Ben: I thought it was really hard to read too. I had the same initial reaction. I started to think about it a little bit though and it occurred to me that it's possible. I don't know who wrote it, but one of the distinctions between Sera and Ben that really jumped out at me in the book is that Ben gets at the very least a little more leeway from society than Sera gets. Sera is met with a level that is just vicious at every single instance, from things as innocuous as when she gets into a cab and she's got a couple day-old bruises and they just go right in for the kill, each one of them, and at least there are some sympathetic public encounters that Ben had where people look at him, like the woman in the bar, for example, and she gives him this kind of longing "oh you could be so handsome and dynamic but it's so sad to see you in this state I wish you were a better" and Sera virtually gets none of that. Not even from the buttoned-up guy from Pennsylvania, he treats her like a dog. And it's really a brutal experience, and when you look at it from that lens, it's possible that Sera is falling back into the habits and the patterns when her old pimp shows up...we talk about it in law, *constructive* versus *actual*.

She has an *actual choice* but does she really have a *constructive choice*? Because society is telling her every single place she turns: tourists, cab drivers, johns, everyone, is just going in for the kill with her. So does she really have this ability to choose her own way? Or is she just trying to do the best that she can under the circumstances she finds herself in? Or is that at least that's how she's conditioned?

Bob: Clearly her greatest value is her will; she needs to survive. I thought throughout all that's been described here, I found her to be incredibly inspiring, and impressed by her ability because her view here is the opposite of Ben's, who is resigned—his cards are dealt and he's going to die. She's fighting.

She's fighting every challenge. She stands up for it, so every time…. what were the names?…The couple she befriended?

Rob: Oh, the neighbors?

Bob: Yes! Her response to that was uplifting. She wasn't letting them define her, so it was actually a fairly impressive show of individual strength. And clearly she was bothered by all of that and the whole piece about her feeling the need to be validated, but I think that she had a sense of self-worth that Ben doesn't have.

Ben: I think it's a really good point to mention that little episode with the neighbors. I think that really illustrates this notion that she really just didn't have options, she didn't have realistic human options because even in a situation where she crossed all her T's and dotted all her I's with these neighbors, they were the aggressors, they were the instigators of this friendship. They refused to leave her alone and she kept her guard up as best she could, and finally, after a violent episode, she had one human moment and literally the next morning, got the hell out and we better not ever see you again.

Rob: And the husband would leer at her too.

Ben: And it's like, wow, this is not a person with legitimate safety nets.

Dave: So going back to the idea of strength. So you have three characters, right? There's the triptych: three characters that play off each other.

Alok: That's how the book is sold but, the pimp, he has a really minor role.

Dave: Right. He has a minor role as far as space but what is his response? What happens to him? He becomes paranoid, right, and he loses his mind. I think it highlights the strength of Sera. Again, there's this inner strength that she has that, it's almost like she's walking through fire and both Ben and Al, they're you know, they're...

Bob: Yeah, but don't you think though that with Al...his challenge now, is having to move on from who he was? He had everything going for him, he had the money, he had all the power, and we're seeing Al now at a point now where everything is changing for him, and the way he describes it, it all happens fast, all these bad things including getting old, getting old was his, that was sort of like the pivotal piece. What we're seeing in him is he has no ability to go back to where he was. Sera is at that same point in her life now, she thinks that she can do what she's doing now forever. Big question, the way I see it, when she's talking about how she's kidding herself or what the truth is, all the things that she's failing to confront, part of it is, that she thinks that she can do this forever, but she can't do this forever, and she's at that point in her life now...what are her options? Is it the Ben route or the Al route? Neither of which are close to ideal to her. So when we leave her in this book, she's the last one standing in terms of how is she going to approach this pivotal point when she's hitting 30 and she has chosen a line of work that's not going to sustain itself, and what are her options? How does she continue her number one goal of surviving and living now with more limited options?

Alok: I agree with all of that, but I think by saying that how Sera's powerful or how Sera's is empowered...misses some of the point of what the author is trying to say, which is that not everyone makes the right choice. We are saying these are the right choices and these are the wrong choices, because that's what mainstream society sees — that's how we frame it too, but I think what O'Brien is saying is that both of them, Sera and Ben are deeply damaged people, as you know, but they are making a choice to stay this way. That's their personality. With her I can't pinpoint specifically, there are pages in there or there are paragraphs she talks about it. She has this real need to have companionship but, she also has this real need to be sexual with strangers. That's what's stopping her from just quitting and working at McDonald's or something and quit taking chances. She has this real need to be a certain person. Again, she has this need to have sex as a successful career, and he also has this real need to be an alcoholic and die soon. And I think that's what the book brings out is this sort of really neglected aspect of life, and that some people are just wanting to be that way. It's a choice, not fate.

Rob: Let's talk about suicide as far as suicide that is instantaneous, a bunch of pills at once, or a shotgun to the head, compared to a suicide that is planned and executed the way Ben does it. And why do you think he picks the latter instead of the former when he decides he's going to exit the world? Why wait 100 days and do it this way? Any thoughts on that?

Ben: I thought it was such an interesting question that you ask because the notion that he's committing suicide...it's obviously alluded to and it's sort of front and center of this notion of slow-motion suicide. I didn't necessarily in my head put it in those words though when I was reading, I just read it more in terms of the brutal self-destructive pattern of an addict that's leading, that's leading to a one-way street. We don't know where it's going and he accelerates it and accentuates it in such a dramatic way that it does come across as a live-action suicide. And even Sera who has "agreed to the bargain" her sense of revulsion at certain moments, that I just can't watch this, I can't watch this person who I've learned to care about do this to himself. But I think it's really interesting if you want to bring in the notion... just to think about this in the context of suicide and just the mere notion that maybe for me this idea that you automatically associate suicide with this moment...as opposed to what Ben did which is this progressive decline, even if it's rapidly accelerating over the course of addiction.

I'm not a psychologist and I don't treat depression but I've known people who have committed suicide and those episodes caused me to think and to read a little bit and try to understand these issues. And I think it's the same sort of thing that you were talking about, Alok, which is that there's power over the individual in either situation that maybe isn't as easily classified as the rest the world would like to look at it as "oh it's just a choice at that moment". And you know of course by saying this, I'm generalizing across all acts of suicide, I don't mean to be doing that, but I do think that the concept of suicide is something that's a lot more complex than a moment as opposed to a process.

Alok: No, I don't think that this is only the act of suicide or an active choice. I think it's more "so I am going to do this thing that I enjoy very much" and the downside of that is that "I will die at the end, but that's OK because I like drinking and there is a difference between that and "I hate what I'm doing and I want to kill myself."

Dave: That's the sense of romanticism that I referred to...it's a projection...it's a fantasy, an alcoholic's fantasy where you are projecting, "how would I want to die?" So if I'm going to die, I'm going to continue to drink, drink myself to death with this beautiful woman tending to me, a woman where there's no demands on him. She cares for him, she's a sex worker and that she protects her feelings, her emotions, and just when he knows that she's getting a little close, he breaks it off, but then she comes back and she's there as this angel.

Rob: Excellent points. This is a good time for a break.

Leaving Las Vegas as Existential Literature

Tanya Pilumeli

-Thus it amounts to the same thing whether one gets drunk alone or is a leader of nations.

- Jean-Paul Sartre *Being and Nothingness*

- The sublime act of selfish selfishness that she is prolonging; the basic loneliness of her humanity, and the knowing and accepting the conditions of that which has been shown to assuage it. Sera's not living up to any agreement, she is simply living.

- John O'Brien *Leaving Las Vegas*

It is true that we as a society do not as a whole support Jean-Paul Sartre's idea that a drunk and a hero are of the same value. No one has been told as a high school graduate, "Please, dear, go off and get drunk instead of getting a job if it suits you." And as a whole, we all agree that society would fall apart this way. Yet, that is not what Sartre means. As the father of contemporary Existentialism, he is defending the philosophy that our choices are always our own, and our choices are the only thing that creates meaning for us in the world. In contemporary USA, with so much opportunity and comfort, so much choice, how is it we have so many lost and searching people, so many people without meaning? John O'Brien, in his 1990 novel, *Leaving Las Vegas*, would argue that it is because people need to be true to themselves by constantly choosing to be their true selves amid their anguish and despair. While Ben's alcoholic spiral downwards and Sera's unorthodox and unstable lifestyle may seem like a depressive diatribe with a tragic ending, it is really a postmodern endorsement of Sartre's Existential Humanism.

A French author and philosopher who came of age during the German occupation, Sartre was concerned with human awareness in the world and picked up on the ideas of Husserl and Heidegger. His ideas eventually became the foremost thoughts on man and his relationship to his meaning for living. Existentialism boils down to the idea that since we cannot control all of the things outside of ourselves, life is not rational; it is absurd and uncontrollable. Because of this, we only have our own selves to rely on, and so we have only our own choices to create our meaning. The only path to meaning, and therefore freedom and value, for Sartre is to continually be true to our own purpose without relation to how the current outside reference frame judges our path. Yes, this will cause anguish and despair, and that has been popularized as the Existential Angst, but Sartre would say you can't make that go away, so why try? Once accepted, the anguish of being leads to a sort of enlightened contentment.

Although *Leaving Las Vegas* is filled with horrible situations and ends with Ben's death, the message throughout the whole text was that even these people, this drunk and this whore, and maybe especially these people, have found meaning and value amid the anguish and despair of living. Beginning with their names, we are led through a modern Existential proclamation. Ben, or "been," as the past tense of being, and Sera, which in Spanish means "will be," encompass the range of being that we encounter in our lives. Even Gamal Fathi, or "conqueror of beauty" in Arabic, has his role in exposing the importance of finding meaning and value in one's choices by being true to one's self while also being responsible in our relation to others.

When we first meet Sera, she tells us right away that life is "a long, hard, painful ride in a car filled with chums" (4). And the first line of dialogue is Sera asking Ben, "Hey! Are you alive?" (5). At this point we don't know that the drunk she sees and passes by is Ben, but it doesn't matter. It is the question, are you alive, that becomes central to the book. What does it mean to be alive? We find out right away that she is a prostitute, "and she is a good thing, good at this thing" (5). She realizes her purpose, that of helping men unburden themselves and find their own identity through sex. And she enjoys this sense of meaning, even though it is a controversial one. "That's a real fact, true on any level. Then and there, absolutely, though perhaps exclusively, she has value" (32).

As Sera goes about her unorthodox life, she flashes back to moments with Gamal, her pimp, before he finds her again and tries to reconnect. But Sera has chosen to move to Las Vegas from L.A. for herself and gained a sense of courage because of it: "the pain is really only as bad as the time spent on it" (20). Victor Frankl, the Austrian psychologist, concentration camp survivor, and Existentialist writer of *Man's Search for Meaning*, writes that "life is never made unbearable by circumstances, but only by lack of meaning and purpose" (Frankl). Even after her brutal encounter with the college boys, she finds a way to find value in her life: "She is still alive...nothing about this can put her down. There was never any question." (33).

It is clear that Sera believes that staying alive amid her anguish to fulfill her purpose of "working," even if her job is not one many would connect value to is her true purpose. In her apartment when not working she even sees the appliances as more meaningful than her because the fridge is "happy" and "secure in the knowledge that it is doing its job," and she is envious of the TV characters because they are in a "series of cruel plays about people with purpose" (44). But while Sera is able to gain value and meaning while working- "she must work. Sera must work; this has always been her weakness-" (45) she still cannot realize her value and meaning at all times, just in being. And that is where her Gamal and Ben come into her life. She realizes, as do all the characters, that although one's true meaning and purpose come from realizing the true self through action, the validation of that truth and meaning can only come from someone else. Sartre says in his essay Existential Humanism that "he recognizes that he cannot be anything…unless others recognize him as such. I cannot obtain any truth whatsoever about myself, except through the mediation of another. The other is indispensable to my existence, and equally to any knowledge I can have of myself" (Sartre EH).

Gamal has come to Las Vegas to find Sera. His name implies that his meaning is not just to be, like Sera and Ben, but to conquer another. This is a common theme in Existential literature. Since "there is no reality except in action" according to Sartre, man "is therefore nothing else but the sum of his actions, nothing but what his life is" (Sartre EH). For Gamal, losing Sera to her freedom means losing his identity as conqueror. He has lost all his wealth, beauty and glamor and believes that if he can command Sera, "she will be his, and he will be him. As it was" (45).

In the past, in flashbacks, Sera feels that the key to finding meaning while not working is to tell her story: "Sera…wished that she had someone to tell the story to…no…that wasn't it. She wished that someone would listen to her tell the story" (25). Now that she is working for herself, by her own choice, she sometimes finds it hard to accept some of the darker truths about herself. Yet, until she can she will not be able to truly grasp her meaning and value: "She cannot accept that she needs to be, at least at some deeply hidden level, or even in some insignificant way, accepted, validated like a parking ticket, punched" (32). When Al steps back into her life and takes back her choice and she turns her trick for him, she realizes that when that choice is gone she is "nothing" (57). O'Brien even represents her state of being as "( ) ( ) ( )" (57).

Unlike Sera, Ben seems to accept his purpose and give value to it without hesitation. His journey to Las Vegas and disposal of worldly goods has meaning and purpose to him because, although to everyone else this way of living is a wasteful act of uncontrollable laziness, he himself sees it as a way of being true to who he is. Sartre says that there is no universal morality except for the morality of being true to your value and "consequently every purpose, individual it may be, is of universal value" (Sartre EH). Ben goes about his life fully understanding that he is a drunk with limited time left. But he is deliberate in his actions. He doesn't care that he is an alcoholic. But as O'Brien writes, "It's not what the story is about" (68).

As a parallel to Sera, he also connects with his fridge and other inanimate objects around him. Just like them, he sees himself as "an object of his own device" (68). His actions, from walking and making sure he doesn't leave anything behind for people to have to deal with to picking a bar and how he can pay respectfully, are all planned and meant to responsibly facilitate his purpose as a drunk in relation with others. In his journey to Las Vegas he also encounters the question of validation. When the bank clerk asks him, "Do you need a validation?" he thinks "that sounds pretty good to him, but even if she meant it, she wouldn't know where to begin" (79). He then imagines the bank teller in the form he most desires, a prostitute dripping with bourbon who tells him, "'There! See! I have a purpose. I have a place, and a value'...How very strange that would feel, to be so well understood" (81). And here we see what Ben is searching for still for his validation is embodied in Sera.

Sartre believed one of the main ways to be validated by another was through sexual encounters. Since "there is no hope except in his action," (Sartre EH) it makes sense that an active union with another that understands our purpose and validates it is the most potent way to fully consent to "being." O'Brien shows Ben's attitude towards prostitution while he is still in L.A. and has yet to meet Sera: "to him there's no better meshing of social and biological functions than paid sex. It's always gratifying, leaving him quite pleased with himself and with the world in general" (85).

As he prepares to move to L.A., he moves closer and closer to his meaning and his purpose by deciding to get rid of two things that an Existentialist would say hold man back from attaining his true

41

meaning: time and possessions. By removing himself to Las Vegas, he will be able to buy his liquor at any hour without a thought to the hour. By getting rid of his possessions he is killing two birds with one stone; he is leaving nothing behind for others to take care of, and he putting (placing?) all of his meaning into his actions and not his things, "for he cannot bear to see waste, much less generate it...So separated from him and each other, his possessions no longer have a story to tell. They are reduced to elements, building blocks of a modern American existence. No longer parts summing into a whole, they are without collective meaning, an eraser mark on the page of his life" (96).

In opposition to Ben, we have Gamal Fahti, the conqueror of beauty, who has is trying to validate his identity and meaning by conquering Sera. After she had left him and he lost everything, "rather than be not-Al, he stayed and did everything he knew to become Al again. But he couldn't...There was something that he had defeated long ago; it was away in a different place, and for that reason, he thought, he could defeat it again" (111). When he first finds Sera he believes he still has existential meaning even though "he now admits to himself his recent doubts about his power over her. Clearly it continues to exist; she remains his possession" (106). He then uses his language to continually reaffirm this. He tells her, "you have been lonely" a few times and she believes "she *has* been lonely. His voice makes sense" (106). And as he mounts her, he affirms his being: "so am I" (106). He can smell her fear and this confirmation of his power over her is all he needs. But it is clear right away that things are not the same. As Al tries to have sex with her he is unable to cause her pain or to consummate his desire. There is no validation: "He can – and will – do whatever he wants to her, but he can't hurt her. Anyone can do anything to her; she couldn't care less" (116). As Victor Frankl wrote, "the one thing you can't take away from me is the way I choose to respond to what you do to me.

The last of one's freedoms is to choose one's attitude in any given circumstance" (Frankl).

After this it is a downward spiral for Gamal for he has lost his power over her and therefore any meaning in himself. He becomes paranoid and reclusive and loses all interest in living: "everyone stares at him, yet no one knows him – he knows no one" (118). Sera meets Ben and they begin right away to validate each other: "she is pleased to have impulsively identified herself to him...It felt... like the first totally self-motivated thing she has done in days...He adores this girl because she has a valid reason for liking him: two hundred and fifty dollars" (127). Yet she still hasn't broken entirely free from Al. It isn't until Al slaps her and she likes it that she feels she has a key to the lock on her freedom. She starts to realize that if she doesn't fear anything about him, she chooses to not care and therefore keeps her freedom.

As Ben and Sera get to know each other, "a vacuum, long unaddressed in sera and always fundamental in Ben, is being looked at and considered" (142). They are able to look at the non-rationality of their individual ideas of meaning and hope that through the other's acceptance they may gain the validation they need to continue "being." His plan is to die, hers is to stay alive, and she enjoys helping people. She asks him to move in and declares "I am my own boss," in which she realizes she has regained her own volition (145). As she meets with Al she hears his voice muffled, through a door, and it no longer has control over her. He "sounds strange to her: Al, but not Al."

With Al entirely out of her life, she is free to explore her relationship with Ben. Ben tells her that he is in love with her because he is a drunk and she is all right with that, and he feels fine with her being a prostitute and knows that she needs him to understand that. Sera realizes that "he needs her, and for that, she loves him" (165). Though they still don't have sex, their relationship is sexual in

43

nature, and as they move toward their goals, act out their purposes – his drinking until he dies, hers staying alive no matter what while also helping Ben – they continue to live small moments that create meaning just by 'being.' They go shopping, go out together, and take a mini vacation, albeit in very unique ways that correspond to their situations.

As Ben realizes he is near his end he decides he needs to be alone. She does not want this and tells him, "this is the one thing you can do for me. I've given you gallons of free will here, you can do this for me...As sick as you are, I'm probably the only thing that's keeping you alive" (184). Ben knows this is true, and it is for this reason he needs to go. So he chooses to bring a hooker into her home to create a new boundary between them, a way for him to choose to keep to his purpose, however irrational it is. When she finally finds him again two weeks later, they finally have a sexual encounter which ends in his death. As it ends, she hears a siren and "when the sound fades it is replaced by nothing, nothing" (188). In this moment "it all becomes clear, how much more deliberate his life was than hers, how he knew the one great trick that she couldn't do" (188). It is as if, in Ben's death, O'Brien is mirroring what Martin Heidegger says in *Being and Time:* "we all die, and die on our own, each person turning toward eventual nothingness...Beyond reaching our own potential there is no purpose to life" (Heidegger).

In the end, Sera is "unaware of. . . the truth in her life" as she "lies awake in the darkness" (189). In another whimsical twist, 'sera' is the Italian word for evening, and it is that American nightmare, that darkness that we all go into that Eliot describes in "The Wasteland," that Sera is left with. She understands enough to know that she needs to stay alive, by working and helping others, by fulfilling her purpose, creating her own meaning. O'Brien leaves us with the image of the dead drunk and the aging whore as living the purest life they know possible, something we all might turn away from as against everything our culture seems to hold important. But as Sartre wrote, "life is nothing until it is lived; but it is yours to make sense of, and the value of it is nothing else but the sense you choose" (Sartre EH).

Leaving Las Vegas Roundtable
Part Two

For part two we invited John's sister, Erin.

Dave: I'm going to read a couple of the questions that Rob phrased really well.

Question 1: He writes "with no textual evidence from the four canonical Gospels, in the 6th Century, Pope Gregory The Great created the archetype of the benevolent whore by proclaiming that Mary Magdalene was a prostitute. Would you agree that Sera has aspects of this archetype? If you agree, does it take away from any of the flesh and blood realism of the character or, for that matter, the story?

Question 2: Did Sera try hard enough to save Ben or does she realize that his fate is sealed and any further attempt is useless maybe even counterintuitively unethical?

Bob: When you think about the story within the scriptures about the one prostitute, it's about who without sin can cast the first stone. There's many elements of this book that talks about being judgmental... about how people react to both substance abuse and prostitution and the dynamic between it was very interesting. The glue that held Ben and Sera together was their lack of judging....their insistence of not being judgmental and remain accepting.

However, I thought John nailed it when he wrote about when she walked into the room and he was with a prostitute, *there are limits*.

There can be limits to being nonjudgmental. This runs counter in a biblical sense. There are limits.

Alok: So I guess I'll say we've spent a lot of our time talking about the main character in the book. I think it's easy to say maybe because the author's life was somewhat similar, the assumption was it was easy for him to write? Then you look at Sera's character and say OK, it's a very different character and still seems realistic.

We've read other books...what was that book? *Submergence*? A female character written by a male writer.

Rob: Yeah, right. Right! Great point.

Alok: The female character in that book mostly comes across as a guy's fantasy, not as a living, breathing person. Sera is real, a prostitute could be written more as a male fantasy, but she is believable.

Rob: I agree.

Alok: I just want to acknowledge that it is done well in this book. Now whether she fits *Madonna/Whore* complex or not, I think she's transcended that. She makes the end of Ben's life meaningful and provides companionship during his last days. I think she was very well written, a very well thought-through character with all the psychology and complexity of a fully-realized character.

She's not addicted to substances, but she is addicted to some form of masochism even though she denies it which adds to the depth of her phycology and complexity of her character.

Dave: Can you elaborate regarding her addiction to masochism?

Alok: Even though she knew she was in trouble with those three kids, she still walks through that door...and somewhere else in the book, it says her one job is to stay alive. So she does realize, at some subconscious level, that she's putting her life in danger. Her number one concern is to stay alive which is different than Ben's in the sense that Ben's number one concern is to wind down living.

You can probably spend an hour just talking about her psychological motivation and how she is a very complex personality, even without the parts of the book concerning Ben. The book is so well written... she's much more than an archetype.

Rob: I couldn't agree more. Just because she happens to fit some of the archetype, it doesn't mean she's solely archetypical and I think that she is a full-blown character, beating heart, not just myth or fantasy.

When you mentioned *Submergence*, Alok, if you compare those two female characters, Sera's living, breathing, she seems to have a historical presence. I don't believe the character in *Submergence* was any of these and I think she was just a male fantasy. And even though prostitutes can be drawn with male fantasy, in fact, it may take real skill not to, I don't think that's it at all.

Moving on, the fatalism, Alok, when you said she walks in with the three young boys, I wondered about fatalism in this book too. We could talk about that too if anyone has any ideas. because obviously, Ben is fatalistic. And though fatalism is important concerning Ben, I didn't even think about Sera and fatalism until Alok mentioned it.

Dave:: Right, obviously Ben is fatalistic. Sera, I think that when we talked earlier, we talked about her strength. How many of us would be willing to put our bodies in that much danger? The descriptions wash over you where she's really being abused and many are brutal and not just the rape scene. Whether she being treated roughly during sex or being beaten up. So I don't know if it's fatalistic, it's certainly fatalistic and it's masochistic, it's some sort of role that she's playing.

Ben: The flip side of it, she's portrayed as tough, and takes pride that she can handle these encounters. Her job that is to sexually satisfy some of the most sociopathic men who come her way. These are men who...while she has johns who are the easy Midwestern guy there for a conference, a regular part of her routine is a sadistic, violent creep who's going to get his greatest erotic thrill out of hurting her. And she knows how to do that. She's good at it and she takes pride in that she knows, for the most part, how to handle these creeps and she has pride in her ability to roll with that. It's hard to disentangle... it's hard to disentangle what part of that is from empowerment, what part of that is her own psychological disorder, what part of that is her own being trapped in the situation she is in.

Bob: I also saw her need for connectedness. We sort of focused on the violent side of her world. But she talked about the gift that she was... the moment of this short encounter when she was giving something that, maybe just for a second, was meaningful to somebody. And it seemed like her whole relationship with Ben was all rooted in offering to mean he was offering her something that she deeply needed, companionship, some level of connection, that kind of even drove her work at times.

Ben: I think that's a great point. To your point, she remarks on several different occasions that she would bring these men to a sort of truest manifestation of, I forget exactly how she described it, or how the narrator described it, but this iteration of hurting themselves was their purest form and it was like in the act or the moment of climax or what not, but it was always with her and through her.

Bob: From Ben's point of view, to the extent that that was important, he lost it all. He lost it all from his last day in L.A., when he actually had an angel, this person at the bar, they were eyeing each other, she seemed to want to connect with him. He had this thought and what does he do? He looks down on his glass. That was his rejection of this element of connectedness that he didn't get again until he met Sera. He finally had this connection to her that was meaningful to him. But I think for her that was her defining thing, it was really her drive.

Erin: I don't have my copy with me, but I always try to talk about John by using his words. The first thing I think we hear about Sera is that's she is a circle, 29 years around, which is so great. John does that on purpose: 29 is a prime number, divisible only by itself and the number one. Conversely, Ben is a straight line, and a tangential relationship occurs. That's the first thing that's important about Sera.

Then there's her name. You all noted her name S-E-R-A—and I hope I don't botch this—but I think that's a truncated version of Seraphim, the word for angel.

The most important thing that Ben owns is the Rolex because he values time more than anything else, which is what everybody misses. Then he sells the Rolex for $500. And a transactional thing occurs, the money that he got from the Rolex is the money he uses to buy two hours of a beautiful hooker's time. That's an important component.

The other component that's really significant from a religious standpoint is that this relationship is never consummated. There is this dreadful ejaculation at the end of the novel, but sex for Sera is only with other men. And I'm not going to go on and on about the symbolism with that, but those are the four biggest components of her character. And the other thing to note, only because I carry John with me, is about the rape scene...if John were here...he'd be like: *Oh God, everyone's gonna call her a hooker with a heart of gold*...so he put the rape scene up front to dispel that notion.

And that's the first place we see her because her number one concern is to get back to work. And I think that was, from a writer's point of view, that was his device to say she's gonna do that first because she's not a hooker with a heart of gold, this is her job, this is what she does.

John would not have approved of Mike Figgis putting that rape scene at the end.

Rob: Absolutely!

Erin: Because it changes her character...

Rob: Yes, it does. That's a great point. One thing I want to talk about and I wanted Dave to either clarify or challenge what you said. You talked about the romanticism of the book and I take the opposite view. You know we've talked about Bukowski and some of these other writers, and college kids and others will read Bukowski who was a horrible drunk and they'll have these great quotes from him like one is you know, I'll paraphrase, the bartender says Bukowski's alter ego in his books and the films based on those books Hank Chanaski. The bartender will say something like Chanaski "why don't you get a job?" and he, Chanaski, replies something incredibly witty like "a job? It takes a real man to make it without working" and all these romanticized versions of what a drunk is. I think, with Ben in LLV, we have somebody who has to get one-fifth of vodka down and vomit it out, to get a second fifth down just to stop his hands from shaking so he can sign a check.

That kind of is de-romanticizes or un-romanticizes what an alcoholic is. And so I'm on the fence about the romanticism...and have a hard time seeing the fantasy aspect. I find it's very unromantic with a large "R" or very an unromantic book. Let's talk about realism, you want realism, if you come to a state where you're gasping for air and vomiting and trying to get enough alcohol in you just to be able to function, that's about as unromantic as anything I can think of. So I just wanted everyone's thoughts on that notion?

Alok: I was on his side, now I'm on yours! *General Laughter from the Group*

Ben: I felt the same way. I felt pulled in both directions. When you started out this session describing your (Dave's) view I agreed.

Dave: There's a certain charm to his character, and there's life in his character and while he's describing that, the vomiting, and I've had friends who talked about before they went to bed, they would pour a dog bowl full of vodka, so when the woke up they could put their face in it because they knew they would have the shakes so bad they wouldn't be able to hold a glass.

But when you see them drunk, it's unbelievable, they're the life of the party. Here, when I'm using romanticism, there's a certain attitude like fuck it, I'm going balls out towards death...And it is a sort of youthful energy to his suicide. It doesn't feel like it's the end of the line, where it's, it's not a guy you can see at a bar who is basically staring into the bar and they can't put two words together.

Ben: He does bring up the notion a couple different times of the character example of the person who's lost their mind, likely as a result of addiction.

Dave: Right.

Ben: I think that's a good observation.

Dave: It's like the guy who's driving 140 miles an hour on a winding road ready to just plow into a tree, not giving a shit, but you're still drawn to the guy that does it. There's a certain romantic allure, you're being drawn to people, even though you wouldn't want to be this person. We all have struggles with our day to day lives but here is somebody who is checking out.

Bob: The moment for me though that pulled at me was when he calls her, he's in his last moments and he says something along the lines of I'm sorry I tore us asunder or something like that. Because he said that whole thing, given her feelings for him, his going with that prostitute, was his separation, the only possible way he could have helped Sera deal with his ultimate demise, allowing him to go, is to do that. It was like tearing them asunder was one of the more generous things he did for her. But his expression of that showed just how much he was pained. He had something special, he did it for her but he's sorry about that. This pain that he was expressing, all had to do with his feelings for Sera which to me was really a wrenching kind of moment.

Erin: There is an element that's really discrete here and again I think of John and I think of vice, and I think of place, and this is Las Vegas and it's John's Las Vegas so we go back to the year 1989. Here's a pyramid, and you'll believe it. Here's the Eiffel Tower in

Las Vegas and you'll believe it. You go into a casino and there are no windows...and all the flashing lights...and the free liquor is available 24 hours. Reality is suspended, and so when we have a drunk and a hooker falling in love in Las Vegas, we can't take our eyes from these characters. You cannot take your eyes from these characters and I don't think the same thing would be said if they were in London or Los Angeles or anywhere else. I think that's one of the things that creates this kind of push and pull you all are talking about.

Is it romantic? We're all being duped by this grand illusion that is Las Vegas. I just think it's a component at play with the reader and everyone else. Anyone who's been there — and if you haven't, it's just a place unlike any other and everything's a façade and always has been. Yet we really want to believe, whether it's romantic or not. We want to believe these two characters. If they're a drunk and a hooker we don't care, we still want to believe them and believe in them.

Rob: They're both very humane and I think that Ben, the world as it is, being apart of this world, that it is he just can't handle it, beyond the disease. He just can't, he realizes that this is not a place for him.

Which leads me to, I want to talk about the title of the book, *Leaving Las Vegas*. There is only really, so Ben leaves Las Vegas, but if you don't know how the book ends, how he leaves Las Vegas, you somehow would think that maybe he escapes it, and he does but only through death. Does anybody have any thoughts on that? Ben?

Ben: You know I like to take the floor if I had something to say, but to be honest with you I felt a little bit stumped by that question, in the sense of like I wasn't sure how I felt about it. I have almost the same copy of the book and I think the cover on it, the cover image, interacts a little bit with your question, it just makes me have this sense of, you know, I'm not really sure where you're going with the question. I don't really have much to say about it.

Rob: I think I really like this cover and I haven't seen it before, but it does let the book stand on its own. And I think it deserves to, anybody else has any thoughts on this?

Bob: Interestingly, the only one in the book, from what I understand, the only one that leaves Las Vegas is Al.

So what I said earlier about Al in terms of being this character who reached this point in his life where everything has changed for him, getting old. He's had to make this drastic life-changing...I mean he's no longer who he was, he comes to Vegas for this purpose and it's not worth it, he's leaving cause this isn't working. He's got to figure it out someplace else.

Think about where the book leaves Sera, in this state of contemplation now, as she goes to bed and she's the only one that hasn't left, in one way or the other, and what does that mean for her? She has two examples of how you leave Las Vegas. You either go out Ben's way or you go out Al's way, neither of which are particularly attractive. Where's her life going to take her? She's not going to be able to do this forever.

How does she survive? What is her next move? How does she reinvent herself? How does she continue to survive? How does she leave Las Vegas? You know how's she going to leave that's different than the two examples she's witnessed?

Alok: I don't know if I could put it better.

55

Rob: Exactly, well said, Bob.

Alok: I don't know if I am just reading too much into the title, but I believe the whole story is about getting Sera to leave Las Vegas. She has seen, as you said, various ways to leave, including permanently or to go on a bender and...so the optimist in me wants to believe that she left Las Vegas on her own terms, and had a happy ending. But if you look at everything that happened in the book you know that's probably not what happened.

Erin: Phonetically it's perfect, it's the most perfectly phonetic title you can imagine, Leaving Las Vegas, and when it was born in John's head...that was it, for sure.

Every one of the points you bring up is valid, you know you can interpret it in any way you want, all the characters—everyone there for that matter—they all leave Las Vegas in one sense or another. Something else that's very important, the title includes the name *Las Vegas*. Further to the point that I was getting at before, that is really a hint: this was a fantasy way to end his life. You're not going to go and buy a few cases of liquor and die in a hotel room with a beautiful hooker. When you're an alcoholic, that is a fantasy. Trust me, my brother drank very hard to try and ingest enough alcohol to kill himself, and he couldn't do it.

I think the title is just indelible and I'll leave these comments with an unfortunate piece of information, after the Las Vegas shooting, the headline, at Huffington Post was Grieving Las Vegas, I just wanted to hurl.

Rob: I saw that I was very...very...just speechless…that Sheryl Crow song is a whole other thing, that he was furious about that Sheryl

Crow song because he knew one of the guys that used the title to write the song and John was supposed to get credit and never did. So it's a legendary title right now, but all your points are valid, but the fantastical component of the story, it's right there.

Rob: I went to Las Vegas because I'm writing the introduction of this book, and editing along with Dave so I wanted to see it firsthand and I had the book with me.

I re-read the book again while I was in Las Vegas and the descriptions that he has, and I even have a picture of the 7-Eleven and we'll probably use that somewhere in the book, but walking through these casinos he just absolutely nails completely the feeling of what it's like.

The only difference now is that people are looking at cell phones and then at the slot machine and other than that the description hasn't changed, and at the time I was thinking, if he's looking at leaving Las Vegas, and in Ben's mind if Vegas is a metaphor for existence or his world with the experiences that have made him, him, then I can't blame him for exiting it...for leaving Las Vegas.

With that, we're going to do the reverse of our book club and we'll just have a closing argument so to speak. A final statement maybe Erin can have the last word. Instead of going from my left maybe this time Bob I'll start with you, especially since you are somewhat familiar with closing arguments (*General Laughter*). If there is anything that we missed that you thought was pertinent, or whatever, or if you're done that's fine.

Bob: No, I'll just go back to my original comments...I do remember seeing the movie at some point years ago and I really appreciate the opportunity to have read the book. This remarkable writer, when I talked to you even, when I mentioned that the ending it was very, a gripping story.

Given my personal work, during the course of my career dealing with folks that present themselves with, on this underside of life, it rang true and what other greater compliment can you pay to a writer than to say that. The amount of experience that I have and to have seen people struggle with addiction or being into prostitution, all of that, this rang true so, I appreciate the opportunity to have read a classic in this fashion, so thank you.

Alok: I think for me the best part of the book, I know you said it's a fantasy and it is, but it shines a light on the reality of life for many people. And so it is a fantasy but also isn't. I think is says...it shines a light in a way that's really nonjudgmental. And so you see all these really terrible acts, the rape of Sera right at the start, how pathetic it is to sort of be an alcoholic and crave it all the time and making all these arrangements... and that part about putting dollar bills in the front pocket because you might be so drunk you can't reach in your wallet to pull the dollars out. And all these other things Sera has to experience and even the pain that is inflicted with Al and the knife and all this other stuff and—that could easily have passed judgment on such behavior or actions…but it's not presented that way, it's just presented in a very nonjudgmental state. This is what some people go through and this is what some people's lives are. And it's not right or wrong, this is just how it is. And some people may romanticize this their own lives, but here I'm telling you how it really is...and for me, that was the best part.

It's definitely a masterpiece of writing by representing the lives of these people that we generally don't see displayed realistically on TV or in books or in the movies to this extent.

Dave: There's a reason we don't see lives like this represented on TV and movies, It was the particular genius of Mike Figgis to cull such a good movie fron this material. I mean in the hands of a lessor director most of it would unwatchable because you lose O'Brien's voice. I think it's a true testament of how good the book is that you can go back and forth and you can think of it in these different ways, these different prisms: Romanticism and Realism. Different characters' point of view and the way they all interplay with each other...you can see the fantasy aspect of it. You can see it as an alcoholic's fantasy, of how they would want to go out, being tended to by an angel while they are so bitter drunk right til the end with there still being a stark realism to it. It doesn't go in to parody at all. So you know, and while we talked a lot about the author more than we ever do, I think it's very apparent that somebody had to walk through hell to write the book. That's what comes across to me. You know it's one thing to read great novels and you can have a writer that can write a Roman history and then do an academic history and they're all great writers and that's so believable, but there is something so true it's almost memoir that comes through and I don't think it's unfair to him to say that. So, and I think it will stand, and I think it certainly a classic, that will stand the test of time.

Ben: This was the hardest book I ever had to read. And I say that at the risk of exaggeration but it's the honest to God truth, you can ask my fiancé, I◉ve plowed through over the course of last week and with each prolonged reading, I went in to a more intense state of living with the intensity of the suffering that was being described in it and the intensity is really the keyword and a lot of books try to get after suffering but there was just something about the way that this book was written that was so gripping to me and it really hit uncomfortably home for me too. My name is Ben, I grew up in Cleveland, I was born in L.A., a lot of his descriptions of Los Angeles are familiar to me. I come from a Scots-Irish background that has had its share hard living individuals. It was a really hard book to read but not only because of the subject matter and the way that it was described, the unvarnished way it was described, but also because I just thought he was so remarkably gifted as a writer and it was just intensely sad to me that we don't have more from him than we do..

Erin: I just cannot thank you all enough for inviting me and for spending time with John's work. I profoundly appreciate that. And all of your very articulate comments are right on track. Every interpretation of this book is appropriate. It's always about the writing to me—and the devices, which he nails. There's is no exposition. Writing 101: "show don't tell," right? John never does because he walked the walk and every single detail is nailed: the 7-Eleven, the Lemons, Bars, Cherries of the chapter titles…That is how it's done. And so his expertise, that's where it comes from.

I hope that I haven't been long winded and I hope my presence here didn't make anyone uncomfortable. It's been a pleasure to talk about John's work. In the wake of the Leaving Las Vegas phenomenon, people would call me and write me. I got a 15-page letter from some guy in Ireland "Oh John's my hero," he said, "I'm gonna join him." Then one woman contacted me saying that John made a pass at her at a party 15 years prior. I mean I've heard everything. I've heard it all so I'm pretty tough about it because John's work speaks for itself and John speaks for himself and it's unassailable in many ways. Anyway, people aren't always thoughtful when it comes to their comments about John, which is why I appreciate all of you. And I just can't wait to see everyone's efforts in the book.

That which begins will also end

Dorrian D'Apice

I exist on the best terms I can. The past is now part of my future The present is well out of hand.

--Ian Curtis

Two darkly written and beautiful characters struggle to face their existence in John O'Brien's hauntingly self-fulfilling prophecy of a novel, Leaving Las Vegas. Within their struggles to exist, Ben and Sera meet each other at their most raw, their most vulnerable, yet most committed selves. While the story of a prostitute falling in love with an alcoholic whose sole motivation is to "leave Las Vegas" by drinking himself to death seems hopelessly full of despair, there is an ultimate, and counter-intuitively, life-affirming message in that both characters can embrace now wholeheartedly. One could argue that both characters are victims of circumstance, but they are ultimately both empowered by the way they fully embrace their existence.

Sera is determined to control her own life in Las Vegas. She went to Vegas to escape a violent past she had with her pimp, Al. "(Safely on the bus to Las Vegas and thinking back for the first time, Sera was amazed at the timeliness of the elevator's arrival. Ten, five more seconds might have changed everything (italics mine). She could still be there, maybe giving another sponge bath to that smelly accountant whom Al sent her to the night before. But it went her way. . . for the first time, she did leave, not just the room, but the apartment and ultimately the city... she felt wonderful to have done this one thing." Al will, eventually, follow her to Vegas, and try to regain what he lost with her disappearance.

Ben goes to Vegas not to escape the dominant factor that controls his life- alcoholism - but to embrace it without reservation. He wants to liberate himself from the shackles of time restraints and his daily existence. He goes to Vegas with his entire life savings in his wallet with the intention of not having his day dictated by time. When he sells his Rolex, O'Brien, masterfully, doesn't explain the metaphor. He has complete trust in his abilities. A lesser writer may have been compelled to make sure we got this unburdening of time, maybe even feeling the urge to, for example, burn the calendar that he would happen to have with him. Ben unloads his Rolex as easily as he runs up his credit cards, sells his car, the symbol of time is weighty but to hammer the point would have been overkill, the act speaks volumes.

Most bars elsewhere are closed. In Las Vegas, however, Ben drinks whenever he has the need. He is aware that he will leave Las Vegas by drinking himself to death, and there is no other motivation for his actions. As Ben takes off for Las Vegas, his intent is crystal clear. "For him, there is a grim thrill in this crystallization of intent. . . This tapestry which he is never unraveling really told a story to begin with; it was always non - figurative and woven without volition. Very drunk, but well fueled with purpose, he turns to the more detailed task of purging the very personal things." Before Ben determined that his essence would be to leave Las Vegas by drinking, we may safely assume, his life lacked purpose. As soon as he fully commits himself to the idea of dying in this way, it is easy for Ben to sever ties with the existence he had. His life might have spun out of control up until this point, but he realizes that he can control the end. Ben's end is entirely a construct of his "volition."

According to the existential maxim existence precedes essence, Ben and Sera were given lives to live. How they choose their existence is up to them, according to the maxim. They choose to fall in love, and they have committed to honor each other's choices of character. When Ben tells Sera that she cannot ask him not to drink, it is clear that they accept each others' true essence. The fact that they each know the essence of the other from the onset makes the dynamic authentic. This authenticity expedites the sense of connection between them. As Ben and Sera discuss how she works, how she picks up clients and schedules them, there is a moment of honesty, nearly unbearable honesty. Together they stroke the silence. "I hope you understand that I'm a person who is totally at ease with this. You are not an oddity to me. In fact, I feel rather akin to you. Please don't think my apparent indifference means that I don't care, I do. It simply means that I trust and accept your judgment, your inclinations. What I'm saying is: I hope you understand that I understand." With that, Sera tells Ben that included with the rent is a complimentary blow job. Ben requests that Sera never ask him to stop drinking. In the same way that Ben understands Sera, she obviously, understands him.

This is an example of Sera as the empath. She even expresses this empathic capacity when Al - her former pimp - slaps her across the face after a slow night on the Strip. "And she likes it. She doesn't know why but it tastes like the key to something, and she likes it... she also remembers the tears, and how each cut into her was really a much deeper cut into him... unbelievably, she wants to go to him, to help him. She wants to absorb his pain." Sera feels this very same empathic impulse toward Ben, and this is clear when she extends the invitation to stay at her apartment. She further illustrates she wants to absorb some of Ben's pain when she buys him several gifts before moving into her apartment: a shirt and a flask. When Ben opens the flask, he says, "It looks like I'm with the right girl...I must say I'm rather impressed that you would buy this for me. I know it wasn't done with some deliberation. Funny - how you did what I would have done." It is not that Ben and Sera encourage the worst in each other; it is instead simply, that they passively accept each other as they are.

While the intent to end his life is Ben's sole motivation, starting a relationship is an unforeseen complication. With most of his possessions gone and having what remains of his life savings in his wallet to burn, interestingly, the details of his ex-wife and his divorce are intentionally vague and murky. His wedding ring is "Rendered barren of its original significance, and it is the only tangible relic of a marriage long-gone by. . .They parted with no malice: she regretful, he drunk . . . He has never deciphered what the chicken was and what was the egg; his drinking encouraged her resentment, and her resentment accelerated his drinking." Ben's essence is clear. He must end his life and maintaining any human connection, or material possession will only detract from achieving his goal. Viewed in the context Sera is, indeed, a possible, even more so a probable, complication.

Nietzsche's theory of Eternal Recurrence is echoed throughout this book for me because of both Ben and Sera's cyclical patterns of existence. Essentially when faced with the materialistic approach of Eternal Recurrence, people ask themselves if they want this existence again and innumerable times again. "Would you not throw yourself down and gnash your teeth and curse the demon who spoke thus? Or have you once experienced a tremendous moment when you would have answered him: 'You are a god and never have I heard anything more divine.' If this thought gained possession of you, it would change you as you are or perhaps crush you. The question in each and everything, 'Do you desire this once more and innumerable times more?' Would lie upon your actions as the greatest weight. Or how well disposed would you have to become to yourself and to life to crave nothing more fervently than this ultimate eternal confirmation and seal?" Sera willingly chooses her existence day after day; she enjoys the freedoms of this existence, carved out be her choices. Ben's demon of eternal recurrence is his alcoholism, an inescapable illness, not a character defect. He realizes that he will never be able to escape this demon, so instead of running from it, he embraces it fully by orchestrating a perfect ending for himself and the demons who will leave Las Vegas with him.

At the end of the novel, after Ben shatters a bottle of bourbon and gets shards of glass embedded in his skin, Sera asks Ben to see a doctor and he will not because that will undoubtedly interfere with his intention of dying. Sera says, "Let's face it. As sick as you are, I'm probably the only thing keeping you alive right now." Ben knows there is truth in that statement because Sera is the sole connection he has maintained. In an effort to sever from this '"complication" Ben recruits a hooker who has had "a lot of use" to take care of his needs at Sera's apartment. Sera enters the scene and tells Ben that there are limits. Because of their intimate connection, she feels that this is an ultimate betrayal. Earlier in the novel, Ben comments about liking women with mismatched earrings. Sera replies, "Well then, let's hope we don't run into any tonight. I do expect some sort of loyalty here. Just because I fuck for money doesn't give you cause to start picking up women and leaving me looking silly." After Sera catches Ben with the hooker, she feels like she was indeed left looking silly so she kicks Ben out of her apartment. Twelve days later, he dies with her watching his dead eyes stare toward the ceiling.

Shortly before this, with the end near, and his only goal of leaving Las Vegas, a poetic way in his mind: "'Quiet,'" he said, resting his hand over her mouth. 'Try not to be so consumed with the future.' However, Sera had not felt the future at all, for it was not until that moment, laden with his words and redolent with his prescience that she too knew what would come to pass. It all became clear how much more deliberate his life was than hers. How he knew the one great trick that she could not do camera and how she would fall in love with him every minute, every second, over and over again come for the rest of her life."

After she watches "his lifeless body grow cold on the hotel

bed," Sera returns to her apartment where she undresses, brushes her teeth, and lies awake in the darkness. Their relationship has given both these characters a way to "Let go and fuck God."

Consider this striking phrase, after all we know from this story... "Let go and fuck God,"? Is this Ben and Sera's radical line-in-the-sand stand for choice? Their declaration of independence? Their inalienable rights to exist in the way they choose...to build their existence moment by moment, disregarding judgments from societal norms and family expectations and all expectations in between? Is there a more radical way to develop self than to "Let go and fuck God"? Is this their rebellion?

Better

Burning Out: John O'Brien's Quest for Better

Matt Marshall

If there's a prevailing emotion, a prevailing pressure, that John O'Brien's characters face, it is that of being trapped. The fact that they have, by and large, ensnared themselves, is of little help or consolation—on the contrary, the anxiety is only increased because the imprisoned serve as their own jailers and yet struggle to find the key that will unlock the cell. In the face of an ever-more-terrifying outside world, pressing in with its absurd, obscene demands (economic, social, sexual, etc.), O'Brien's characters retreat inward, burrowing deeply into a private bunker and then finding themselves unable or unwilling to retrace their steps back to the surface. We join them already in the pit, the gate swung shut on their particular ring of compulsive hell.

O'Brien's first novel, *Leaving Las Vegas*, takes us inside the author's two favorite prisons, alcoholism and prostitution, first separately, then as a shared space once Ben, the alcoholic, and Sera, the prostitute, come together. The testosterone- and alcohol-fueled gun nuts of his second novel, *The Assault on Tony's*, are the victims of an outside force—pandemic countrywide rioting—that requires them to hole up in their favorite bar for a couple of weeks. And though the force in this fantastical tale comes from the outside, it is used as an allegorical springboard to examine the characters' internal conflicts. The painfully awkward Carroll Mine of O'Brien's third novel, *Stripper Lessons*, is caught up in nightly returns to a strip club. The fact that Carroll is not cognizant of his compulsive behavior (and, unlike other O'Brien male protagonists, is not an alcoholic or even a drinker)—shutting himself away in a highly controlled, ritualized environment—makes his entrapment no less real. Yet through his struggles at the club and at work, where the long-sought-after "Solo" file folder is found, in the end, to have nothing in it, there's a sense that maybe Carroll will learn from his experiences and come to see his forced ejection to the outside world as a positive step. *Better*, the second book written by O'Brien but the last to be published, manages to end on an even more hopeful, if still qualified, note. It is also unique among O'Brien's work in that it seeks not only to dramatize the torment of self-imprisonment but to sketch its very architecture.

The risk of cliché and repetition is acute for a writer like O'Brien who focuses three of his four novels on one particular illness. But the alcoholism that O'Brien portrays is never one-dimensional. His characters are shaped and tormented by a host of competing biological, psychological and social influences. Indeed, intentionally or not (and I'm assuming that O'Brien never strived to be this clinical), his work hews closely to the biopsychosocial model for understanding illness that was introduced by George Engel in 1977 and has challenged the traditional biomedical model ever since, particularly in the realm of psychiatry. But maybe O'Brien is able to explore the terrain of this model so successfully exactly because the model itself is not so clinical.

The biopsychosocial model has increasingly received criticism from psychiatrists and other physicians for this very reason— that it's not scientifically rigorous enough, open to any number of perspectives, all of which might be entertained as valid within the model's purview. Similarly, the predominant disease model for addiction has come under fire from some experts who note that addiction just doesn't share the aspects commonly associated with disease, other than, as psychiatrist Lance Dodes observes, "if people do not deal with it, their lives tend to get worse." Yet O'Brien, writing in the late 1980s and early 1990s, borrows heavily from both models— the prevailing medical thinking of his day—putting it to good use in his fictive worlds. In *Better*, he even goes beyond what most disease model proponents (and the evidence) might suggest by investing so heavily in the notion of genetic causation of addiction. The house that he constructs to constrain *Better*'s characters serves both as a multi-dimensional diagram of alcohol addiction and as an experimental setting to carry out a thought problem. He can feed characters into the structure like hypothetical rats, discovering which doors need to be opened and which need to be closed, which "rats" need to be brought together and which need to be pulled apart (and when) in order to navigate his lead rat, William, through to the improved state of "better." This is O'Brien searching for the *why* and *how* of the imprisoning affliction—not just its *now*—a nuanced understanding that might lead to the titular promised land.

Like addiction, this word "better" is not something easily pinned down. It usually serves as an auxiliary to a directive or indicates some nebulous state of being—a desired destination. But even within these divisions, it occupies a good deal of blurry space. In a directive it can identify a practical obligation (I *better* fill the tank or I'll run out of gas) or an irrational, self-critical one (I *better* get the promotion or it'll prove that I'm a failure; I *better* agree with my peers so they don't reject or hate me). As a destination, "better" can represent an ill-defined state of improvement (things are bound to get *better*) or a more quantifiable one (I was sick, but now I am *better*). But, always, "better" is something of a concession—that is, it is never the "best."

The ambiguity—the striving, shaming, ultimately limiting quality—of "better" makes it a most fitting title for a John O'Brien novel. Like the person navigating addiction, the reader who tries to square this title with the book's content is confronted by a slippery series of hits and misses. On the whole, the title appears appropriate, but it can't be used to fasten the novel to some specific moral agenda.

In presenting the alcoholic condition, O'Brien takes a different tack than, say, Malcolm Lowry, that nonpareil portrayer of the alcoholic mind, who gives us a consciousness in real (drunk) time, snaking its way through various depths of incoherence. Instead,

O'Brien employs a layering, collage-like technique, intermixing the biological, psychological and social components of the alcoholic life (and of being human, in general) to produce a caged, muddled effect. The resultant aesthetic puzzle never quite adds up; it is a labyrinth that ensnares both O'Brien's characters and his readers, offering no apparent escape. Like the Zone in Andrei Tarkovsky's film, *Stalker*, the landscape of O'Brien's fiction changes according to the mental and physical approach taken by those moving through it. This unsettled quality to O'Brien's work is what gives it substance and, I suspect, what leads many readers to frustration and dismissal. With the possible exception of *Stripper Lessons*, O'Brien's novels simply can't be read as works of pure realism—not if we're to make sense of them. The realistic *presentation*, no doubt, tempts many readers to take them as such, but cracks invariably form in the gloss as the reader attempts to go deeper. At its best, O'Brien's fiction not only manages the balancing act between realism, fantasy and farce, but exploits the ambiguity to steer the reader toward a reconsideration of entrenched ideas on modern life, generally, and on addiction, in particular. While not free of missteps, *Better*, on the whole, achieves this tricky business. As with *Leaving Las Vegas* and *The Assault on Tony's*, reading *Better*'s vodka- and gin-soaked pages is liable to produce the sour-stomach, head-wrung feeling of a hangover, making the reading at times less than enjoyable, infuriating and off-putting, even. But for those who push on, the book rewards with plenty of intellectual grit, applying something of a fateful, naturalistic analysis to the lives of the middle-class "losers" spit out by the American machine.

Inside Out

Like all of O'Brien's novels, *Better* is a bit weird and unsettled. It maintains a surface veneer of realism over an ever-shifting foundation of metaphorical fantasy. Ostensibly, it is the story of five young misfits living in the L.A. home of a rich eccentric named

Double Felix. Yet from the outset, this "reality" is called into question. The two-page prologue ends on an unfinished thought from narrator William ("Then I would have cut them off sharply, stifled my own cue and said,") that, one could argue, casts the entire novel as William's introduction to the unknown neighbors who have wandered onto the driveway—an introduction loaded with that obligation so familiar in O'Brien's fiction, that of justifying one's existence: I *better* explain myself. Is this, then, a meta-novel? Are the housemates that William proceeds to tell us about only figments of his imagination? Aspects of his own character that he's struggling to comprehend? Composites of family, friends, strangers and lovers who have tormented his past and continue to bounce around within his skull? Perhaps. There is plenty in the text that invites such an interpretation, but just as much to convince us otherwise—that William is telling it straight and does, indeed, share this house with the other people in his story. Through William's narration, O'Brien leads us down paths that continually crumble underfoot, only to be replaced by footing no more sure. Shifting in and out of "reality," he portrays the mind unspooling from entrenched psychological trauma, plowing through the kinks, performing the terrible task of getting better.

William is, after all, a severely addicted individual. Like most of O'Brien's male heroes, William consumes alcohol surely as he breaths. And this gives us all the more reason to question his veracity. The ironical-classical fashion with which he launches his tale carries the mark of the cynic, of a man who longs for a life of meaning but sees only the deck stacked against him and those like him: "Start that long climb again, oh hapless paperboy, working your reiterative way up the hill and down the hill, over and over, day in and day out." We are not, clearly, in the redoubtable hands of Homer or Dante. William may be looking to summon an epic of Sisyphean import, but the tale is doomed to bog down in the mundane routine of everyday existence, in the sunbaked lounge chairs and TV-controlled couches of anesthetized America, in the compulsive depravity of the alcoholic life.

The story begins at nightfall as William retreats to his favorite chaise lounge on the house's communal deck. His rationale for selecting this bed might equally explain why he has chosen to remain in the house, while also serving as an overall assessment of his life: "Now I find I am here for reasons that I can no more control than I can understand." Nevertheless, the story that unfolds, relating the events of the following day and evening, and ending with the house's destruction by fire, will be just such an attempt at understanding and control.

The psychological struggle begins at the most uncomfortable spot for an O'Brien character (or, at least, for his male characters): *outside*. William has been spending his nights on the deck for a few months by this point, and, while this decision may be beyond his control (among the things the book's shifting biopsychosocial palettes call into question is the existence of free will), it is, nevertheless, a last-gasp effort not only at survival, but at a future. Even among O'Brien's characters, who typically suffer from some degree of agoraphobia, William is a special case. Having lived in the house for three years, he hasn't moved beyond its limits for the last two. So his insistence on sleeping outside on the deck is a significant, if small, step toward his recovery. However, it is not a move without psychological risk, as O'Brien makes clear by laying William at the rail of a house set on a cliff overlooking the ocean.

The outdoors is a strange, dangerous place in all of O'Brien's novels. Characters venture out only when necessary, usually when they're trying to get from one enclosed space to another, and even then they prefer to travel by car—a mechanical cocoon, as it were—that will protect them from any threatening foreign elements. Walking outside is the strangest activity of all, signaling a stubborn independence that doesn't align with—and may even be an outright

73

rejection of—our modern, automated society. In *Leaving Las Vegas*, walking is one of the great joys that Ben's alcoholism has robbed him of. And for Sera, walking the strip late one night gives her the opportunity to slow down, change her perspective and see Las Vegas for the repetitive false promise that it is. To venture outside in *The Assault on Tony's* is basically to commit suicide (a *quicker* suicide, that is, since remaining indoors will get you sooner or later, too). The scene where the men undertake a mad recovery mission to their cars is among the most tense—the most gripping—of O'Brien's oeuvre. In *Stripper Lessons*, Carroll decides to brave a patch of West L.A. on foot and nearly gets run over by drivers who can't fathom why anyone would be so foolish—so suspect—as to travel under the power of their own legs, thereby disrupting the regulated flow of traffic. Not only has modern civilization divorced humanity from the natural world, O'Brien seems to argue, but it works to enforce a code of unquestioning adherence to its automated life.

Stripper Lessons also examines the exclusivity of being indoors, with its various sects, levels of privilege and gatekeepers. At book's end, Carroll, now banned from the strip club that has been the center of his existence, stands outside in the club's parking lot, forced to endure some light mocking from two unrestricted patrons just before they, in good, automated fashion, "suck into door." The extreme hyphenation of the book's final word, "In—side," emphasizes the divide between those who are in and those who are out. Which side are you on? Adopting the prevailing societal view, most O'Brien characters assume that it is better—safer—to be inside, an assumption they often pay for with their lives. *Better*, conversely, promotes the benefits of living outside, despite the terror, positing such a life as a possibility for even the most damaged among us.

But to get there, *Better* first divides the preferred inner space into additional subsets of exclusivity. Each tenant in Double Felix's house has a private room, complete with a private bath, private phone line, private bar (of course), and a private balcony that is walled off from neighboring balconies. The changing cast of lodgers, most of whom receive a personal invitation from Double Felix to stay in the house (although, some, like Maggie, simply choose to linger after a house party), remain in the house for as long as it suits them. William indicates that guests have been known to stay penned up in their rooms for days, barely acknowledging the others. Double Felix, himself, rarely emerges and doesn't allow groups to congregate in his private room. Exclusivity, O'Brien shows us, quickly runs toward isolation. A character will, however, enter another's room from time to time for drink, talk or sex. The most regular of these couplings are the Morning Vodka sessions, replete with drunken philosophizing and homoerotic tension that William and Double Felix engage in daily from 5:00 to 6:00 a.m. on the balcony off Double Felix's room. For group activities, there is a large, shared living space at the front of the house that Double Felix refers to as "the big room" and "the place from which we commence our satellite activities." Though this is apparently the gathering spot during parties, throughout the day covered in the book there are rarely more than two or three characters in the room at any one time. A long hallway connects the big room to the seven bedrooms, the shared deck and the kitchen.

The description of the house and the way that William and the rest of the cast move through it recalls the architectural understanding of the human mind as argued by archeologist Steven Mithen in his 1996 book *The Prehistory of the Mind*. Mithen proposes an evolved mind constructed like a cathedral, with a nave of general intelligence and multiple connected chapels of specialized intelligences, each open to its neighbor and sharing information back and forth. In the Double Felix house, William is the conduit that allows much of the information from the residents' private rooms to become known in other rooms as he moves from one to the next. There are even a few peculiar instances in which William relates the interaction between others in rooms that are shut off to him—he admits not witnessing the scenes and no one else tells him about them. Odder still, his narrative strays three times into the thoughts of other characters, twice into Timmy's and once into Maggie's, each time passing briefly through the mind of Laurie. These curious stylistic choices not only give additional credence to the theory that the entire story is a product of William's imagination but also encourage us to view the house and the action within it as a metaphorical treatment of brain circuitry—and of a rather distressed brain at that, namely William's. When considered as such, occurrences that seem out of place when taken as realism—such as when the courier shows up at the house to deliver Double Felix's roundabout message to William or when Timmy bounces a ball off the big room's outside wall, causing a repetitive pounding noise—become instead dramatizations of a haywire brain with its misfiring circuits, inefficient messaging system and pounding headaches.

Obviously, O'Brien, who wrote *Better* in 1990 and died in 1994, could not have drawn from Mithen's work. But that work itself relied on ideas proposed by psychologists throughout the 1980s, such as Howard Gardner's theory of multiple intelligences, which O'Brien might have been aware of. But whether he was or not is ultimately immaterial. It is, perhaps, even more interesting if we assume that O'Brien had no direct knowledge of these contemporary theories, and yet chose to construct a similar psychological model for novelistic exploration.

What's In a Name?

O'Brien announces his position on the biological causes of addiction through the names he gives key characters, indisputably linking them to biological processes. Double Felix, whom William identifies as a father figure to the others (if a "disgraced" one), is clearly meant to be associated with the DNA molecule. Of Double Felix's house, William says he "would have sworn [Double Felix] built it himself, for it matches him and he it to a degree seemingly beyond coincidence." As the order of the house starts to break down, Double Felix himself pronounces, "I have worn out my welcome in the house I made, for my children have grown to resent me." And since William feels "very much an element in whatever it is [Double Felix] has wrought here," it's hard not to view the two characters as raggedly, but irrevocably, bound—a twisted pair, as it were. The twining wraps even tighter and more twisted when William admits to feeling like he is, somehow, Laurie's father, a role that, by book's end, is all but conclusively ascribed to Double Felix, who in the past, it is made clear, also had a sexual relationship with the teenaged Laurie. Given this link, William's pursuit of—and eventual sex with—Laurie becomes rather disturbing. Throughout the book, most notably with the oft-repeated suggestion that William and Double Felix are lovers, O'Brien keeps the identities of William and Double Felix spinning like a thaumatrope, crudely superimposing one upon the other till the reader is left to wonder if they are, indeed, separate characters or rather different iterations of the same man.

The disease model of addiction, which has predominated for more or less the past 50 years, and to which O'Brien certainly seems to subscribe, is summed up in the National Institute on Drug Abuse's definition of addiction: "a chronic, relapsing brain disease that is characterized by compulsive drug seeking and use, despite harmful consequences." With prolonged use, so the theory goes, the drug hijacks the circuitry of the brain, disrupting its natural functioning and conditioning it to value the drug above almost everything else. Today, addiction is understood to be a fairly fluid thing, played out in degrees of severity along a "substance use disorder" spectrum, as detailed in the Diagnostic and Statistical Manual of Mental Disorders (DSM-5). But in the days of *Better*'s writing, the accepted premise was that a definite-but-invisible line existed between drug "abuse" and addiction. Once a person crossed over that line, he or she was forever locked into the disease of addiction, whether continuing to use the associated drug or not. (One of the more absurd tenets of this understanding, one that thankfully holds less sway today, is that addiction, even if treated, continues as a progressive chronic disease. Like a demon, it patiently lurks within the recovering addict, building its awful force, waiting to strike anew—more powerfully than ever—should the afflicted be so foolish as to pick up the bottle or the needle again. If an alcoholic with 20 years sobriety starts drinking again, it was said, that person will experience the symptoms of a disease now 20 years advanced—it will suddenly be as if the alcoholic had never stopped drinking!—a terrifying, if incomprehensible concept.) Yet while the existence of a line between abuse and addiction was not in question, its location could never be definitively situated. Being addicted, you simply understood that you had, at some point, tripped that invisible, devastating wire and fallen into addiction, the gate slamming shut behind you.

While O'Brien doesn't write specifically of such a line, he does give us a scene that appears to mark William's passage into addiction. It comes on the morning after his thirty-fourth birthday celebration. Too drunk to drive, William pays for cabs to get everyone home, leaving his own car parked at a bar down the hill, which is visible from the house's elevated vantage:

> Double Felix, glad we'd had a good time, wanted to send me down for it in a limo, but I turned to him and said I really didn't want to leave the house that day and not to worry about the car. I remember him squinting momentarily, smiling and turning away. He stayed out of sight until the following morning when he came into my room at five a.m. and invited me to have vodka with him on his balcony. By the time I noticed that my car had disappeared, Morning Vodka had become a regular conversation hour for him and me, though my car's probable disposition never did come up as a topic. Since then I haven't missed a single hour of vodka with Double Felix, nor any of the other twenty-three as a guest in his house each day.

As I've argued, the car, for O'Brien, is one of the crucial tools for the person who means to participate fully in modern society. To so cavalierly abandon your car, as William does here, to reach a point where you no longer have any feelings of attachment to your car, is to make a bold retreat from society and its fast-paced, automated flow. That William abandons that life for the equally regimented life of addiction shows that he is now completely in thrall to his (addiction-ready) biology. In keeping with the disease model of addiction, he has crossed over the invisible line of no return, surrendering to the prison of addiction as sentenced by his genes. Whether or not this is a clinically accurate way to understand addiction (though, as far as I know, all theories of addiction accept that genetics play some role, if only in increasing a person's susceptibility), it is, certainly, what it often *feels* like. And by making that feeling of imprisonment so central to his fiction, and by presenting it so unflinchingly, O'Brien gives us an emotional insight into addiction that science cannot.

As with William and Double Felix, there is also a biological link drawn between William and his lover, Zipper Allele, who stays in the room next to his. "Zipper allele" is a term lifted directly from genetics. Alleles are alternative forms of a gene that influences how a gene is expressed (e.g., skin pigmentation). In a zipper allele, genetic information is misread for some reason, resulting in a different gene expression than might otherwise be expected. "Zipper and I are nothing if not in harmony," William tells us. And yet theirs is a relationship that has no context—no meaning or footing—in the outside world; it is "firmly rooted in this house," firmly rooted, that is, within DNA's double helix. William recognizes that, unlike himself, Zipper is not resigned to remaining in the house forever. She still has "a real life…a future, a concept too painful for [William] to consider." That he ultimately finds himself at book's end on the outside with Zipper, the house in ruins around them, is a good indication that he is, at last, on the road to recovery, for he will finally need to consider his future, reform his relationship with Zipper and return to "a real life." Yet he is still clutching the vodka bottle, so this is hardly a done deal.

Although Zipper has been William's most steady sexual partner, theirs is an open relationship, and like everyone else in the house they do not confine themselves to monogamy. Throughout the book, we witness a number of sexual pairings, which, like much of the action, don't pass the realism sniff test. For one thing, *so many* pairings occur within the space of this one day. William sleeps with both Maggie and Laurie, and makes a weak attempt with Zipper, one that is driven more by routine than desire. (Reinforcing the notion that William is at the whim of his biology is the fact that many of his sexual couplings are, and have been, the result of suggestions or deliberate setups by Double Felix or Zipper Allele.) Timmy and Laurie also hook up, leaving the house, oddly, to do so, as if driven by some instinct that forces them to copulate elsewhere. Maggie, in addition to screwing William, nearly surrenders to Double Felix, as well, telling herself, "I better fuck him now," a self-diminishing directive meant to calm the upset man. (O'Brien's female characters often surrender in this manner, conditioned to think of their worth primarily in terms of the sexual pleasure they can give to men.) Similarly, William, in trying to explain the odd attraction he feels toward Laurie, tells Double Felix, "I'm not sure how to approach her, so I guess I've decided the thing to do is fuck her—for lack of a better idea." Interaction between the characters commonly operates on this base level—more microbiological than interpersonal—a notion that William reinforces by suggesting to Double Felix that "Maybe what I really want is to fuck [Laurie] with your dick. Maybe I'm no longer interested in anything that hasn't first been signed, soiled, or seeded by you." William's actions are, that is, driven by his DNA—they are not a product of his *will*.

The nonchalant spontaneity of the sex also sets it apart from reality. In *Better* even the sex is automatic. Couples come together with the inevitability of porn actors set on a course of metaphorical adventure, giving the novel, at times, the feel of an X-rated and rather depressing episode of *The Love Boat* (which, as we'll see, is just what O'Brien intends, if primarily for reasons unrelated to biological dictates). Just like on *The Love Boat*, characters in *Better* have few reservations about hopping into the sack with one another. The difference is that those aboard the good ship Double Felix are also standing in for biological processes, mimicking happenings at the cellar level. O'Brien's sister, Erin, has written about the genetic imperatives underlying *Better*, arguing in The Los Angeles Times that "Double Felix's house was a model of the first stage of procreation." Throw misread DNA (in the character of Zipper Allele) into the equation, and it doesn't bode well for later stages of procreation nor for the health of the organism produced.

And, indeed, failure of the organism is exactly what we see. Besides coming together, lodgers at Double Felix's house also pack up and leave during the book's eventful day. They couple and divide and then one of them eventually splits. Timmy is the first to go. Then Laurie and Maggie exit in quick succession. Finally, Zipper and William are forced out as the Double Felix structure self-destructs. Perhaps O'Brien's biological allegory goes even further than this—a reader with sufficient scientific knowledge might be able to draw additional comparisons between the characters' various pairings and divisions and those that occur on a microbiological level. But regardless of how faithfully O'Brien's mirror to the cellular world functions, he clearly means for the action in the house to be seen through a biological lens and for the reader to consider the metaphorical implications of that vision.

William's own name is the final component of O'Brien's biological name game. Timmy and Dennis, the "rivet broker" that William knew briefly in the past, both call him Bill, suggesting that Bill was the name William used before entering the Double Felix home.

O'Brien leaves it to us to form the other common nickname: Will. (As Jorge Luis Borges instructs, chess is the one word prohibited in a riddle about chess.) Casting William as Will positions the novel as a battle between body and mind, biological destiny and free will, fact and fiction. And it leads us to some additional questions. How much agency does William have? Is he the master of his actions or purely a puppet of biological or environmental forces? And what does it mean at the end of the novel when William is no longer under Double Felix's command, but instead answers to a Zipper Allele who no longer carries any metaphorical baggage but is now simply a woman? For each of these, O'Brien's fictive experiment points strongly toward a lack of personal control—the Will in *Better* is a slave to forces outside and within.

The Love Boat

Aside from its similarity to the structure of the mind, the Double Felix house, with its all-white color scheme and balconies and deck overlooking the ocean, also bears a resemblance to a cruise liner. So an additional metaphorical reflection is created when, in the midst of morning doldrums, William flips on a TV in the big room and comes upon an episode of *The Love Boat*. The storyline he finds particularly interesting revolves around Captain Stubing, who is being honored with an "outstanding private citizen" award by an organization of practical jokesters called The Rhinos, a group that, in addition to hijinks, engages in "a lot of good charity and community work." However, when Isaac, the black bartender, is selected to introduce Stubing at the award ceremony ("through a random pin-the-tail-on-the-crew-member type improvisation") the Rhino members get a bit uneasy, with their leader telling Stubing that Isaac "is not exactly Rhino material."

William switches channels at this point in the program and gets caught up in a local talk show. By the time he remembers *The Love*

Boat and switches back, the head Rhino is already departing the ship with a "lesson-learned look" on his face, swearing to Stubing that things within The Rhinos are going to change. All is again well, though William has "missed something important." Having realized too late that he was wasting time on the talk show, William ended up missing the complex and unpleasant (at least by *Love Boat* standards) business of confronting and correcting a moral blind spot. Not coincidentally, such stressful quagmires are just the sorts of human interaction that addictive behavior is meant to bridge. Having, no doubt, missed or avoided similar moments in his own life due to his drinking, William can only return to the grandiose, romantic idea of his spoiled epic in order to make sense of it all:

> I marvel at Captain Stubing's abilities; the man is truly an epic hero. I want to ride *The Love Boat* to all its romantic ports of call, I want to do something nefarious—perhaps fuck a fifteen-year-old girl on its starboard deck—confident that I will be, nonetheless, digested by its facile morality.

This is the dream of every addicted person, I suppose: to not only have the compounding misdeeds, embarrassments, legal troubles, and other messes wrought by addiction magically swept away into a feel-good, sitcom dustbin, but to have life sail along that breezily in the first place, negating the very necessity of the addiction coping strategy. When all foibles and failings are set right within a 60-minute window—and to the automatic reassurance of a laugh track, no less—there's no time for feelings of helplessness to take hold in the psyche. In the real world, however—the world that William's story may be a part of or may only be a reflection of—there is depression and parents and bullies and lovers and nighttime and daytime and morning and evening drinking and hangovers and incest and paperboys biking up and down hills on quixotic quests to win impossible trips to imaginary Hawaii. There are futility and failure and family and fuck all. We are conditioned to trust in the automated flow of modern life—in a life that will stream along as nicely as it does on TV—but in reality, cars too often jump the track. The nefarious act William contemplates committing on the starboard desk is, after all, hardly random: the notion of having sex with a teenage girl is lifted directly from the lived experience of the twisted William-Double Felix pair vis-à-vis Laurie.

O'Brien is keenly aware of the conditioning effect that television has on American life. (We can only imagine what he might do with today's social media and smartphones.) Seen through a biological lens, the "big room," with its wall of TV screens, sometimes all turned on at once, showing the same program or different ones, might be thought of as the brain broadcasting received stimuli. (The only other visual entertainment in the room is, appropriately, a collection of erotic murals produced by a former guest.) Yet the room also serves as a microcosm of our society, with people lounging nearly lifeless in front of the glowing screens, soaking up the inanity, then going forth to act out what they've absorbed. O'Brien makes this clear near the end of the book when the fire breaks out. Having unnecessarily shouted an instruction to Zipper, William reflects, "I guess television has disinclined me from a normal speaking voice under such circumstances." Further, the novel itself moves along like a fatally sick TV program, its narrative eroded from having been played out over and over again, like the worn content on a VHS tape or the misread genetic information passed down from damaged generation to damaged generation. Ray Bradbury and George Orwell famously explored similar notions of TV's power to hypnotize and indoctrinate—to socialize—in *Fahrenheit 451* and *1984*. But here there's no easily delineated line of revolt, no authoritarian state to fight back against. You escape from the house and then what? The house, after all, is your own biological architecture. Hell, O'Brien seems to be telling us, is not so much other people, as it is for Jean-Paul Sartre's imprisoned trio in *No Exit*, but rather the "people" we've internalized. And how do we get away from them?

The Great Double Felix

Continuing with the literary comparisons, *Better* might even be seen as a depraved rewriting of the novel that more than any other sings the tragic romance of the American Dream: *The Great Gatsby*. Like Jay Gatsby, Double Felix is a youngish man of unexplained wealth who draws partiers and other freeloaders to his grand oceanside house, seeming to revel in the gaiety of his guests, while keeping himself tucked away, consumed by the desire of recapturing a lost love. Here, however, that love is not only pedophilic but, likely, incestuous. This is *Gatsby* long after the champagne has gone flat and the hero's sacrificial blood has been flushed from the (gene) pool. Though the American Dream has long been exposed as a vapid, obscene fantasy, it continues to be sold across the country, spreading like a virus through the automated pulse of the nation's TV screens. Going back West won't save you from it—William and friends have taken that tack to its limit. As O'Brien makes more explicit— farcically, ridiculously explicit—in *The Assault on Tony's*, America has reached its closing time. Some 60 years on, the green light of *Gatsby*'s East Coast reflects in the "unnatural blue" light of *Better*'s neon bar sign stationed just off the Pacific Coast Highway. As seen from the Double Felix house, the sign blinks no promise of riches, no dream "so close that [one] could hardly fail to grasp it," but instead signals the inevitable descent into self, into a consuming depressive state that will forestall any action not approved by the diseased mind. It announces the *death* of dreams.

Yet just as TV spreads this disease, it also picks up the slack, providing readymade roles for us to fill. O'Brien envisions a society commandeered by the "facile morality"—the automatic rails—of TV life. Read as a work of realism, much of *Better*'s dialogue and plot come off as unconvincing. Read as a piece of TV mimicry, they're spot-on. Take the sex scene between William and Maggie:

Wordlessly I plop down next to her on the couch, almost too close. She grunts, and we watch TVs awhile, though I don't recognize the program, a videotaped sitcom.

"Get your pressing matter taken care of?" she finally says, but in a voice more monotone and less sarcastic than the words themselves.

"Yep. Thanks," I respond, and she looks at me for the first time.

"Drink?" I ask as I rise to make one for myself.

"Uh uh. Not everyone's a fucking drunk, Willie."

"You're right. I'm sorry," I say, sitting right back down.

My body is telling me it's time for a drink, and if I don't answer soon there will be hell to pay. This will all fit in nicely here; I'm in the mood for some pain, a hurdle or two.

She eyes me suspiciously. Abstinence, even the very thought of it, makes me horny.

Pivoting in her direction, I swing my arm over and behind her head and say, "Hey Maggie, wanna fuck?" I think I'm serious, and I have no idea why.

Of course, they do fuck, and in remarkably quick order, just like they would on TV (and just like good puppets who have "no idea why" they are doing it), repairing to Maggie's room to avoid the unwelcome eyes of Zipper Allele (whatever that might mean, biologically speaking). And it's only at the very end of the scene that O'Brien flushes us from the TV auto-comfort—or drags us deeper into its glossed-over sewer, perhaps—by having a stripping Maggie remark, casually, "I haven't showered yet this morning, so I may be a little ripe."

Notice also that halfway through the above scene, William decides that "[t]his will all fit in nicely here." How are we to understand this if not as the evaluation of a storyteller constructing his tale?

Race Lessons

Like O'Brien's other books, *Better* also takes on the issue of race and class in America, unafraid of following the trail into uncomfortable territory. While not as overtly caught up in racial tensions as is *The Assault on Tony's* (where the white men take refuge in the bar to escape rioting blacks and Latinos, sending the nameless Latino busboy out for recon and liquor, watching America burn on TV, with the White House rebranded "Black House" by a paintbrush-wielding mob), *Better* is more pronounced on the subject than *Stripper Lessons* (where "the black," the only bouncer in the book without a proper name, tosses Carroll from the strip club that he will never reenter—guiding him, as it were, to the outside, the special province of African-Americans). In the prologue, William imagines that his (presumably white) paperboy is in a competition with "some chubby little Mexican kid" who unfairly gets to pedal his way to "Carrier of the Month" on the flat streets of Fontana. And he envisions communing with the neighbors through a "presumptuous grin of glad-to-finally-meet-you-we-live-nearby-so-it's-okay-in-fact-our-menials-may-know-your-menials." During the day's Morning Vodka gab session, Double Felix compares sexism to "the inability of many well-intentioned white men to comfortably relate to blacks." This is reflected in the condescending recollection by Timmy (the house "dudebro" before such a term was coined) of a friend's need to pay for a blow job, "from a black chick, no less." And William himself senses a "subtle libidinal superiority...in black girls." He imagines raping Zipper's Brazilian slave grandmother in her "[c]oyly concupiscent" girlhood and the murder she would no doubt plot against him. While William recognizes the "odd construction" of this daydream, he concludes that "my sullied white soul can simply not imagine fucking a black girl and having her not be in control—more a failure of my imagination than a truth of the world." It is, however, a *truism* of the world, and one commonly perpetuated by TV and other forms of popular entertainment. So it's not surprising that this notion of the wickedly powerful, hypersexualized black woman has wormed its way into William's failing white imagination.

Blackness, for William, is also an analogue to his alcoholic drinking. At one point, he expresses a wish to be of "the not-white race, and so be despised and feared…without working so damn hard at it." A former nine-to-fiver with a wife, and, we can imagine, other tags of the stable, middle-class life, William has subsequently rejected all of this and succumbed to the inner workings of Double Felix's house—to his faulty biology and psychology—what some might call his "demons." In this sense, the house is not far removed from the Catholic idea of purgatory, if in reverse: a weigh station for those passing from the conformity demanded by everyday whiteness into the freer world of wretched, savage blackness. This construct is fashioned, of course, from ugly, but very established, American stereotypes—the very types you might expect to find percolating inside a mind nourished by pre-1990 television.

Given all the biological, psychological and social pressures he's facing—and has faced—William feels "incapable of living." He assumes that he "missed class on the day that they told everyone what the big trick is." So, at some point, like most of O'Brien's men, he took to alcoholic drinking to see himself through (to the safety of the bunker). This was William's original attempt at making life better. Such attempts in O'Brien's fiction tend to lead to destruction. But here O'Brien chooses to guide his "rat" out the other side of the alcoholic maze. This passage through addiction may not hold up under medical scrutiny, the scientific metaphors may not transfer well to the lab, the psychosocial pressures of race, class and TV may themselves be facilely presented, but the book succeeds in capturing the sense of imprisonment that accompanies addiction, with the resignation, guilt, shame, elaborate justifications, ritual, gallows humor, hopelessness, irritation, neediness, obstinacy, anxiety, fatalism and animal survival instinct found therein, all warring against and informing one another to keep the cell locked tight. O'Brien is, after all, a novelist, not a medical researcher. His job is to shift our perspective, not give us cures. *Better* shines a light into the dungeon of addiction in hopes, it would seem, that we might come to think of it in a more rational manner and jettison the powerless—but powerfully enforced and all-too-present—mysticism promoted by the likes of the "sacramentalist sheep in AA," as William brands them.

Sadly, since O'Brien's death, we've come no closer to conquering addiction. Drug overdoses are now the greatest cause of death for Americans under 50. While not direct prescriptions, we can benefit from books (and other works of art) like *Better* that rattle cages, from the inside, as it were, that refuse to give us easy outs, that refuse to romanticize addiction and recovery, but force us to address the affliction's full, ugly complexity even when considering what it might take to make ourselves better.

A Discussion about *Better*: The College Students

Max O'Neil
Cassandra Jackson
Melissa Nahra
Anna Powaski

Anna: Let's start just by getting everyone's overall sentiments.

Cassandra: The first part of the book had many descriptions concerning experiences with drinking and relations with women. In the second half, things started to make more sense and I started to get more into it and began to understand many of the themes.

Melissa: I also thought initially there was too much detail and too much exposition up until about page seventy. During the exposition, I had no idea where the novel was going but while it takes some time for the narrative to get moving I still enjoyed the poetic language.

Max: My first impression was that the main character, William, seems very apathetic and hedonistic and just doesn't really care about anything. He's just in this house for something like three years and he's doing the same thing over and over and over again. And it's almost like he's in purgatory, while the outside world goes on all around him. The house is a symbol for many things but certainly, purgatory is one of them.

He's just relatable in some ways, dislikable in some ways and likable in others. There's an amalgam of all the worst and best parts of yourself when you're reading it and you'll like him while simultaneously disliking him. The dialogue felt genuine and the petulance of all the characters was accurate and it felt real.

Anna: It was a long disposition that also took me a while to connect. When I realized that the point, at least with some of the longer sections, was less about plot or events and more about the characters and their observations and analysis then I started to connect. It's a character-driven story. During much of the description not much happens, the descriptions of the TVs, the bars in all of the rooms, the architectural descriptions all add to the contrived and disturbing world contained within this place.

The character Zipper states in the book that nobody in the book is healthy. Healthy people wouldn't go there. The descriptions were similar to describing a Salvador Dali painting...in the sense that they were distorted and surreal. That's what I liked about the book because of... how can I put it? Real in some ways but also a distorted, dreamlike description of what would otherwise be normal anxiety.

What dawns on you as a reader, and others have agreed with us from what I've read, this is a book about *anxiety*. The story is so heavily driven by characters who have no idea what is going on but the readers think *anxiety*.

This is why so much of this book happens internally, within someone's head. That's the point of so much of the narration...not to describe the outside world but the inside world, inside those walls and inside the mind, William's mind.

Cassandra: Most of the issues in this book except the grand ending are minimal or subtle, no melodrama here...minimal life issues aren't the end of the world. They're not crazy or out of control. There's not much action or anything mind-bending. Because they are inside the apartment or inside the mind, the ideas are fleshed out and perhaps escalated beyond what they otherwise would have been. Everything is so descriptive that it takes on more gravity.

And I think that you know, this might be one of the reasons that our age group was selected to read this book because people our age tend to make our issues, our small issues or basic issues, the end of the world. We twist them and make them more world-altering than they are and make them bigger and more important than they need to be. This is what all of the characters in this book are like...acting immaturely for sure.

Melissa: There is, I think, another reason why William is so detailed in his descriptions. For example, when he becomes really angry and very aggressive at certain points, you get to see his entire thought process. Another example is in the beginning of the book when he first goes to see one of the women of the house...Zipper. He has this way of being very aggressive towards everything. All of his replies are very sarcastic.

I wonder if the reason he gets so aggressive and even so demeaning towards women in the book is related to his alcoholism and that that's the reason he also over explains himself. He's rationalizing. He's supposed to be portrayed as someone drunk. So I think that kind of adds a whole new layer of why he is the way he is. I imagined how it could have been different if he were sober.

Max: Yeah, he kind of just does this back and forth song and dance and since it's all his perspective, you can kind of see how he often is, with his conversation, manipulating...but then he almost always knows that his verbal manipulation is going to fail. At the same time he's demeaning toward women, there's also so much talk about femininity and how he's just envious of the female form and everything, how they feel and how women are the omnipotent ones while all the time, when the women are around him, they can pick him apart and sense or know his thoughts and his actions and the meaning behind them.

But going along with the anxiety, it's more like the after-effects of anxiety where it's just apathy. He's three years at this house at this point. An analogy I thought about is the comfort of a hot bath at the beginning, and how the water becomes tepid. It is not as comfortable getting out into the cold to start over; it isn't something to look forward to.

Anna: What Max said relates directly to what Melissa stated as far as William and Double Felix's alcoholism because, throughout the entire second half, it's almost an hour by hour depiction. For example, the rest of his day after the trauma happens with Lori and Double Felix, when William and Double Felix are drinking their morning vodka and they become progressively drunker, William's intellectual observations don't decrease or dull. William never changes his character or his intellectual thoughts. It doesn't even change when they're spiraling....they're all alcoholics and they're all spiraling but William's intellectual ability doesn't have any demise.

Cassandra: To elaborate on what Max said about women in this book, at first, you know, it comes off like he's demeaning toward them; he's kind of very critical of them or uses them as objects but as the book goes on, he almost glorifies them and elevates them up on a pedestal. These women are mystical beings who can do what they want, they're described as goddesses.*
There was something compelling about these people confined to

one place with tons of alcohol. I know this was a time before reality shows but I was reminded of some of these media hits such as *Big Brother* or *The Bachelor*. This expensive house owned by this rich guy with endless resources, especially booze. It was like the first glimpse of a reality show years before there was one. He even captures, from time to time, the meaningless dramas that happen throughout the day as these shows do. It was almost like he was tapping into some sort of fantasy or, you know, ideas that we as viewers crave without even realizing it. That's why shows like that are so popular now because I think there's something within us all that compels us to watch. Along with all of the intellectual thoughts and musings of William it has this simple side also.

Melissa: Another point at the beginning of the book that struck me as odd about this house is the fact that all these people are able to stay paying absolutely nothing other than having to perform a few duties that aren't even necessary...I think there's this lack of gratefulness. They talk about how they have so much respect for Felix and what he does for them, but we're seeing William three years into this and I can imagine him being very grateful at first, but with time it's just come to be expected. He's just living there and not thinking of how great the benefits really are.

And I think that's an interesting point. He's so caught up in this world and to him it's the real world. In the house we've been talking about, all these problems from an outside perspective, are small. The drama with women, for example, are little issues that grow much larger in proportion within the world William knows. Nothing else goes drastically wrong within the barriers of this house, so even little circumstances with the woman have great significance to him. He has all these privileges but it has become something he's owed or expects, so he's just blind to the outside world after these three years at the house. I think it'd be really interesting to see what kind of person he really was before living this life. I think that would be another important part of this discussion to see who William really was and who he is now.*

Anna: There are some engaging parts of the book when we do get little snippets of the characters' past lives before they were at the house, and because those parts are so limited, and we want to know what got them here, who they were before this confinement, as a reader I hung on to them, but O'Brien wasn't going to fill those parts in for us too much. But every time there's something little about the characters you're super interested in those details. I think leaving us with the lack of answers and the desire to know more was on purpose.*

However, the characters, I agree, aren't grateful for what they have. Look, there are Maggie and Timmy and they hate it. They want to get out. They think that they don't need to be there and they don't need this. This is almost seen as torture or punishment—they're trapped and William is confined within his alcoholism and thoughts. They're here for some reason and although we don't know the exact reason, we sense they weren't valued in the outside world. This isn't a place someone goes when they feel positive about their prospects. They feel like it doesn't matter. Having graciousness is just not even important. They do not exist in a society that values their worth.

Cassandra: The people are desensitized to the outside world. What attracted them to this house? We want to know. We want to understand what attracts people to this? That's why we desire more backstory and understand it's an hour by hour anxiety-ridden drunken play of what's going on in William's mind.

Was every day of all three years like this? He kind of just got sucked into the house. We should discuss his obsessive-compulsive behavior or some sort of disorder because he sleeps out on the porch and he can't even go inside to pee because he feels obsessed and he has these kinds of obsessions that he fixates on, you know? So it's the porch, It's Lori, it's...it's the house that he lives in. All of the obsessive-compulsive characteristics are interesting.

Max: He's an agoraphobic and so is Double Felix. Felix spends all his time in his room-- they're just recluses. As far as the wealth of Double Felix and why he just lets these people stay in this house for no repayment at all...you can assume that he's just obviously a very lonely person, but I think he keeps the people around more for William. Double Felix needs William not to be lonely, but William needs more people.

William is someone who's so lost and lonely and the house is a place where he can feel accepted. The house itself is an entity of its own and it's almost like one of the characters in the book. I made a comparison with purgatory earlier, it feels like time stands still inside the house. They are free to leave; however, it's up to them to make their choices once they leave there. William is misguided, but he bleeds apathy. And everything is just so short- term with him it's always just the next thing, the next thing, the next thing because he's just...he has no attention span. He just reacts and analyzes from moment to moment. He seems to have no desire, no drive. he is all thought,no action.

Melissa: He takes everything moment by moment just because he has nothing else going on in his life. It's not like he has a job and it's not like he really has outside friends anymore.

I wanted to double back to Double Felix being so lonely and letting these people stay for basically no repayment. I kind of compare it to *The Great Gatsby*. Double Felix, like Jay Gatsby, lets all these people into his house not just to make them less lonely but because he's in search of one specific person and in this instance, Daisy's comparable to Lori. Having read Gatsby, I felt I had a better understanding of Double Felix: he's a lonely person and he has money, lots of it, so he's going to go in search of the one thing he truly wants.

Cassandra: The difference between Double Felix and Jay Gatsby is that, unlike Jay Gatsby, Double Felix loves control and when he starts to lose control, he starts to take extreme measures. It's a theory that Felix caused the disaster at the end because it doesn't explicitly say he is the culprit but to me, that's that is where the evidence points.

Anna: That control aspect, William mentions how basically he believes that Double Felix set up Zipper and William. Double Felix is omnipotent and he knows all this is all his creation. William's only rebellion is sleeping on the deck, separating himself from the house. He used to have a life; he used to drive down the highways in a car and he used to do all these things but slowly his confinement became more extreme. He stopped leaving L.A. then he stopped leaving the house and then the porch...his world becomes smaller and smaller and more confined and we are right back to anxiety. The smaller the space, the world, the easier he believes he may be able to regain control.

Max: It's explicit, the control aspect. Zipper had slept with Double Felix beforehand because he knew that William wouldn't be interested after that. Double Felix is manipulative and controlling.

Melissa: So a point that I think is important to note is that this book by John O'Brien is the last book that he wrote before he committed suicide.* And we have a lot to say on that topic.
It seems like some details are left out, was it on purpose? Or perhaps

was he going to insert them later? The book was published in 2009. He killed himself in 1994. From reading reviews online, he has other work where the reader is given more details about the character's history. Perhaps this would have been a longer book and we would have had some of these outstanding questions filled in?

Max: I wondered how much of John is in William? Reading online about John and then knowing that and seeing the way William responds,especially in the ending when he loses the desire to fight the destruction of the house and he even says something about just laying down for an eternal nap. How can it not cross your mind?

Anna: Since we have brought up the ending, I was thinking that maybe we should bring up some points about the symbolism. He chooses to leave Zipper on the back balcony and he walks across the other balcony to try to save Double Felix from a fire and on his way, he passes each room and it is so overtly symbolic the way that every room is described. The way that Lori's room is completely engulfed in flames and the way that Maggie's room is somewhat on fire, the way that Zipper's room had the different colors...and he still wanted to go back and save something in there... and the room that wasn't occupied had no fire at all. It was just dark and empty. Can we talk about William and the symbolism at the end?

Max: I thought the whole book had Biblical or religious overtones in addition to having a modern-day Dante bent. Going through the rooms reminded me of the different levels of Dante's *Inferno*. The rooms are just different levels. As he's shown the different levels, his desire to live transforms.

Cassandra: I feel like if he had a strong desire to live he wouldn't be in the house to begin with.

Anna: Why doesn't he just jump off with Zipper? Why does he go back to Double Felix? When he arrives there's only the firefighter. He doesn't have much of a reaction.

Cassandra: But there's certainly something between William and double Felix. Could it be that William is concerned about his free ride, Double Felix's money and so forth? Could that be why he goes back?

Anna: I don't think that's it. William wouldn't care if he was living out on the street with nothing. I think he wouldn't care if Double Felix expelled him from the house. He doesn't care about the things or the type of life that you would expect that most people would care about.

I don't think he is there just to be a hanger-on.

Melissa: At the beginning of the novel, he talks a lot about how he enjoys having morning vodka with Double Felix. I think that is genuine.

Max: Yeah, but I feel when he went searching for Double Felix it was more about himself than Double Felix.

Anna: The ending comes out of nowhere. The characters seem to be absent. William is having a conversation with Zipper and William doesn't have the reaction that you'd expect when he realizes the situation. It should be dramatic, but O'Brien stays consistent with the character and William doesn't process it as someone else might. William even thinks about how a newscaster may report the scene.
I want to make sure we address an issue that strikes me as important. I believe, there isn't a coincidence as far as which O'Brien book we, as millennials, were asked to discuss. While the characters range in

age, many of them, William included, aren't that much older than we are and at this age, I personally know many young people who have similar underlying anxiety or anxieties.

Consider this quote on page 170, "Even at their most dreadful and tenacious, I have always viewed the conditions of my life as in hand, things to be attended to in due time. Whether or not I affect any changes, whether or not I seriously give it a thought, whether or not I ever I really gaze into the mirror, is all small potatoes to me. For it's only me, only my life, and there's nothing so awful that I can't simply absorb it into my general condition. These matters of my self-esteem are perhaps trivial..." To me, this reflects the type of thinking of a lot of people I know in our generation. This is somewhat apathetic and to a certain extent self-absorption is the lense through which many millennials view themselves, other people, and society as a whole. Again *"There was nothing so awful that I can't simply absorb into my general condition"*. This is basically GAD* that many young people now have even been officially diagnosed with.

Cassandra: I'd like to mention Zipper's character. She comes from a rough background but has somehow come through it with a sound mind. She has many of the characteristics of young women today because though she is strong-willed, she is also sensitive. Laura was the glorified female character but I found Zipper to be more interesting.

Max: Every time William has an issue, it is Zipper who is the strong one for him, the person who can offer him solace and, in the end, she's the only one left. I believe that's why the title of the book is *Better*. My theory is that it is Zipper who is better, better than the rest, in Williams' view, even though O'Brien doesn't ever state that... that's why the title is *Better*. She gives William sound advice...

Cassandra: Yet William walks all over her!

Max: But when he needs solace he goes to her...

Cassandra: That's what many women will do...

Melissa: Since we are on the subject of William and Zipper, there is a small detail of the book but it's something that stuck out to me just because in a work with little humor, I found some here. When William originally goes into Zipper's room, I believe it's Chapter 5 or 6 around there, and he greets her and she's completely naked under the sheets then she willingly gets up and walks around completely exposing herself. She's very, what's the word, she's very *open*. Even though she's completely naked and there's this man in her room she is just herself.

However, then as she's talking to William more and more, and she says she wants to get ready for the day, she tells him to leave the room because she needs her privacy to get ready! So we see that she is not only the one character who has a sound mind, she also can laugh at herself and she is obviously comfortable with herself. She has the most respect for herself too, which is obviously different from the other characters.

Anna: Yeah, that scene is very representative of who Zipper is... Speaking of character representation, a trait I noticed that most of them have in common is how they give so much and then reach a point where they recoil. They are fully unapologetic, walking around nude for instance, or having random sex, blurting out obscenities as Lori does, but when anything approaches a deep and true emotion, then that's out of bounds and either the scene dissipates or the dialogue returns to...sarcasm or this indirect, round-about way of talking about life.

Melissa: Great point. They are willing to give themselves over and then willing to revoke that just as easily.

Cassandra: Kind of like Double Felix and his house.

Anna: That's true.

Cassandra: Why do you think Double Felix did what he did? Because of Lori?

Melissa: This reminded me of yet another Gatsby comparison. When Gatsby wasn't able to have Daisy he fell apart. Without knowing more of the backstory, which we discussed, maybe Felix has more of a past with Lori than we know.

Max: There's an obvious moment of reflection too when he's thinking about the past and it makes him ill. Felix is looking into the expensive pot that he threw up in and watching his reflection. Some wound that he thought was healed obviously wasn't. These expensive possessions mean little to him as shown when he defiles such an expensive object.

Anna: OK, we are to our final point to discuss and we touched on this earlier concerning our ages. The way we are interpreting the book has something to do with our age and lack of life experience. Would we be more sympathetic to some of the characters' shortcomings for example, if we were older?

Cassandra: Everyone's perspectives evolve over time. At our age, we view life with a certain invincibility. That's how the youthful mind works. We are at a point where we are transitioning into young adulthood. We think our way is the right way and even if we think we are taking other perspectives into account, we can't be sure of it. These characters are a bit older than we are but when we make poor decisions like the people in this book we just write it off as us being young.

Melissa: Even though we were chosen to read this book instead of one of O'Brien's other novels because we're young and the characters in the book are young, we are four people between the ages of nineteen and twenty, but we're not alcoholics so we can't always relate to them. There are as many if not more differences than similarities.

Maybe when we have more life experiences and we continue to experience people who have addiction issues or mental health problems then we may have more insight. Let's read it again in ten, fifteen, twenty years and get back together and see how our perspectives have changed.

The Assault
on Tony's

The Assault on Tony's (Liver):
A semi-critical response to John O'Brien's posthumously-published novel

Pat Snee

Three things always crop up for me when reading a novel: 1. What's it about and what is happening? 2. Who is my brain casting in the lead role and is it a story connected by scenes and driven by plot, or is it a novel driven by voice and character that has what we'll call a plot and a setting? And 3. Where in my own experience in life is this thing resonating, or is it?

I devoted my reading of John O'Brien's *The Assault on Tony's* trying not to think that I knew he'd written *Leaving Las Vegas* and that he'd killed himself just as his first novel was about to become the movie that would win awards--of course, you can't not know that, but to dwell on it removes the reader from the actual story (or text as all the hip deconstructionists like to say, if there are any hip deconstructionists), and boy howdy, is this a text to reckon with. (And for full disclosure, I'll add that I am a recovering alcoholic-- liberated is more how I think of it rather than tormented (although I wouldn't wish the detox phase on anyone), and I'm also a guy who wrote plenty and drank more than plenty as I cut my fiction-writing teeth in my twenties and thirties. I even had Harry Crews, the legendary Southern Gothic alcoholic, as my thesis advisor in Gainesville, Florida. It only took me forty years to figure out I needed to stop drinking. On the plus side, I figure I'll get an extra twenty to do something else with, like write this.)

Back to *The Assault on Tony's*. The story is Rudd's, and without an adverbial clause of exposition or palaver, the reader is thrust into a scene that begins: "'How bad is it?' Langston wanted to know, and the truth was Rudd couldn't tell him. 'Not so bad,' he lied."

The next paragraph has Langston prattling a bit about some guy named Miles and where is he and is he down…. "So where is he?"

"'Only shot,' Rudd told him. 'Miles got hit last night during the bombing. That's where he is.'"

Langston then astutely commiserates with the gentle reader: "Damned if this thing doesn't have me feeling six ways of fucked." But halfway down the first page, any thoughts of microwaving a burrito to accompany the read had disappeared, and it was figuring out the six ways I'd been jammed into the maw of this book. But the kindest cut in the maw, of course, comes from O'Brien being one deadeye writer of dialogue and description. There's no lollygagging here, even when the narration catches its breath to give us the omniscience that tells us who Rudd is and how he and his heavily-armed alcoholic comrades--and a waitress and a busboy--got into this place called Tony's during a full-scale insurrection of motley but lethal others at the perfect time to have to barricade themselves inside, deal with it, and measure the stock of liquor and their possible means of deliverance.

Of course, this is just chapter one, and chapter one is entitled "Day 16," so there's a few laps to be accounted for as one presses on, but the chapter ends tragically with one of the last two bottles of J&B being hit by gunfire, and then comically when Langston offers: "'Well that sure didn't sound like Malinowa Raspberry Cordial Liqueur!' lilted Langston, and then he began snoring."

To go back to my three reader things, credit where credit is due to O'Brien. The Assault on Tony's is about alcoholics armed and dangerous hunkered down inside a bar (the bartender is dead, the first casualty) while some spark outside has started a really big *sort of* revolution whose insurgents are, as far as we know, also heavily-armed. Thank God Tony's was designed as a savings and loan building. So the first thing is pretty well on the table early on.

106

The second thing is a bit of a bother. Obviously, Nicholas Cage, having starred in "Leaving Las Vegas" comes up as the first entry in the turkey shoot, but after "Raising Arizona,"I can't think of a Cage movie I like, and I'll confess I've never seen "Leaving Las Vegas." It came out when I was still a ten-beer-a-day guy, and, well, back then paying money to see an alcoholic dying seemed like fluff since I could do it in real time at my favorite bar, although probably not in the same two hour time frame. Art speed is way faster than life speed, but lethal doses are lethal doses.

So I mulled over some other leading men--younger DeNiro, Pacino, Paul Newman, etc. But nah, too much depth and pathos. Then, last week, history threw me a lollipop in Brett Kavanaugh, but he's no lead for this story. Maybe Fenton for him. But then the L.A. vibe came in and I found my head's star for the role of Rudd--Henry Rollins. 'Nuff said. It's my head's movie and fuck you if you don't like it.

The other part of thing two sorts out pretty well. *The Assault on Tony's* is not so much plot-driven as it is *situationally compacted*, and by virtue of the caged setting, the extremity of the characters gets a hefty shove into being what the story is about. And in the constraints O'Brien has built for himself in this novel, he uses his gymnastic abilities with omniscience, scene and language on the sentence-level to, well, kinda show-off. And it's rather enjoyable watching him hot dog it on the page, especially as he performs tricks of omniscience that seem almost preposterous in their concept but somehow find pay-dirt as we read on. One can what-if a lot of stuff about this book, but it's never in doubt that this is one gifted son-of-a-bitch at the helm.

(Sidebar: My ultimate praise of a novel happens as when upon reading *Forrest Gump* or *Catch 22* (among many others)I said: "I wish I'd written that book." In *Assault*, the book doesn't elevate to that, but I spent a bunch of quarters wishing I'd written *that line* or *that paragraph*.)

The third reader thing for me is too easy--John O'Brien may be faking his L.A. World, he may be faking the degree to which people carry guns and ammo as easily as wearing clean underwear, and he may be forcing the sex scenes just a wee bit (given how much alcohol these people are consuming and how few opportunities to bathe they have), but he sure as hell knows and renders how the brain of a big-time alcoholic works. And in case the person reading this is a fourth-grader who believes in a Disneyfied Jesus who Saves *everything*, I'm here to tell you that the bad endings for most of this novel's crew are not a matter of if, they're a matter of when--even if there wasn't the convenient Armageddon outside the bar. Because Rudd, Fenton, Langston, Osmond and Miles have already brought their own bad endings into Tony's before page one. Honestly, the plot premise merely brings those ends with, let's say, more *urgency*.

So again, while the whole story and its setting and degree may not resonate so much for me, the poor souls of these pop-til-you-drop alcoholics have the amp cranked to eleven with 12 strings of resonance.

SPOILER ALERT: We don't know what happens to Rudd at the end. Rudd is gone. He's been shot in the thigh, but he's gone. But I hope he didn't go running straight to an AA meeting, either. After the ER, I mean. Technically, though, this is on O'Brien's sister Erin, who finished the book and wrote chapter 17--about as well as one could have wished for, too.

Anyway, back to Tony's. Chapter two is "Day 1," and we get to see Rudd at the beginning of what turned into the shitshow on Day 16: "Still, it smelled like a two-gun day, and most men he knew routinely carried backups every day....it was a minor joke at the club an hour ago between him and Fenton.

"That was his last drink, and Rudd could feel it was long past time for his next.... Rudd wanted to get a discreet start on the evening's drinking so that when his friend walked in he could say of his fourth scotch something like: What timing! I was just about to order a second." And give O'Brien credit for sheer narrative balls-- he's made a lot of promises in chapter one that the rest of the book will have to keep.

There is no evidence that the NRA or the American Association of Distillers were bankrolling O'Brien as he wrote this (though there is a good bit of evidence unstated in Tony's that O'Brien had grave doubts about guns and about the results of his own addiction), but we readers are a dutiful lot, suspension of disbelief and all that, and well, here we are as the trains that will wreck leave their stations. Walking, grabbing Rudd and saying to him, "No, you idiot!" is not an option. But Rudd is real, and his alcohol metronome beats and he keeps time as he plays his tune. There's nothing not real about his ensemble of drunks when it comes to the need for alcohol and the deliberations about dosing it. But O'Brien is neither sentimental nor celebratory about it--the narrator shares the perfect pitch of the alcoholic and no sheet music necessary. Even Jill, whose economic necessities have cast her as the waitress (and the lone female co-dependent) at Tony's, muses: "...these hopeless desperate men she was stuck here with, she'd pour their drinks and suck their dicks because as bad as they could be at times they were still better than the men on the outside of that door, because there was a certain nobility in their consistency and pathos...despite the fact that every one of was on a greased slide to hell and knew it...." The riot only increases the angle of descent for these mugs.

The astute reader, of course, immersed in this crucible of civil unrest, gunfire, libidinal urges and imminent *delirium tremens*, will no doubt ponder how our damsel manages to maintain a semblance of hygiene for the two weeks-plus and no change of undergarments at hand. And to his credit, I guess, O'Brien handles this exposition eventually, although the idea of "fresh as a daisy" is not in play.

In fact, the only things that probably stink more than these men are their politics and their predilection for killing with their surrogate penises. In fact, it's hard to read this novel in 2018 without thinking that O'Brien has unwittingly and twenty some years ahead of the game exposed a microcosm of Trump supporters (minus the busboy and the interloping liberal pacifist, Carey): White, racist, sexist, gun-toting, alcoholic, and private-club-belonging--there they are. The others, of course, are to blame. And the *others* are very expendable, and my guess is that the line "God bless the Second Amendment" almost made it into somebody's dialogue feed.

The arsenal assembled with its drinking militia here at Tony's is not without some chuckles, either. Osmond, the obese and wimpy one of the lot, carries not one, but two forty-four magnum Smith and Wessons, which he doesn't fire in chapter one's gunplay because, well, he's dead, and not from gunfire.

Fenton, the ingenue of the room, has a forty caliber Glock automatic with a fifteen round clip, or, as Rudd thinks of it, a "plastic" gun. Rudd is a more complex vigilante, as tenderly loyal to his gun brands as he is to J&B: "He fingered his own Walther PPK/S tucked under his belt and was reassured by his command over it. He'd had this gun for over ten years....a mouse gun, the other men derided it as, yet Rudd had taken out his share and more thirteen days ago when it counted most."

It's hard to tell whether the dead others outside are being whisked off to funeral homes, being buried in mass graves, or just rotting in the street outside, but that's another story. Rudd is busy and cogitating after Fenton empties his 15 bullets into something or someone(s): "Rudd instinctively tapped his own Glock nineteen nine-mm holstered on his ankle. Though a larger and more powerful gun than the Walther, the Glock was carried and considered by Rudd as a backup piece."

So here we are with Rudd and the rest trapped in a world full of gun-toting racist alcoholics who are also mostly misogynists and homophobes (and who by story's end all somehow screw the only woman in the story, the lovely but self-doubting Jill--in varying degrees of intimacy and/or consent). Wait. Did I just give O'Brien credit for being prophetic? Let's take a closer look. After it's clear that the cast are stuck in Tony's for the duration, we get a little more insight into the demographics.

Rudd and the busboy are going to go over the rules.

"'Get me some more coffee, Jill.' Then looking at her: 'Half coffee, half whiskey.' Back to the busboy: 'My Hispanic brother and I need to have a chat.'

'You don't even know what race I am,' said the kid after Jill had left the room.

'Sure I do. Not white. Now let's get down to business.'"

The busboy and Jill, in case anyone's keeping score, are not equals in this venture, but on the bright side, that may be a good thing, vis a vis their mortality in this story. At any rate, "The busboy knew he couldn't get back to his neighborhood now, not after the things he'd seen on TV last night....he'd be in much better shape if he were discovered by the National Guard in the company of these white men."

By the end of Rudd's summary of the ground rules, Rudd says something about "being glad they'd reached an understanding. The busboy thought they'd always had one."

O'Brien's gem here has two glowing facets--1. Rudd, having been established as the leader here, is clearly what most readers would call a *douchebag*, but he's not an all-out *asshole*. He's just playing what remains of his gun-toting white male privilege while holding onto just enough of the reader's sympathy to keep the book from being launched across the room. And 2. O'Brien dares to render perspectives through the eyes and minds of the second-class citizens. The full complexities and inequities of America in the waning years of the 20th century are not the *prima facie* plot or character-drivers in Tony's, but they are the ground from which all these poor people spring. And it's pretty clear that rather than celebrating or rooting for any of them, O'Brien is just letting the stew simmer and then boil once in awhile.

There's no point dancing around the need to encapsulate who these alcoholics are and put on the literary equivalent of their character Underoos. I'd argue that Rudd, Jill and the busboy are one's best bets for "round" characters, but O'Brien goes into the heads of all of the others, including the unfortunates Cash and Cards, two others whom we meet over the knife in the back of the man they just killed. But the charter members of Tony's are:

Langston, who as we meet him, is on the verge of the DT's (who isn't?), listens as Rudd and Fenton have assembled what's left of the wrecked dry storage in front of the assembly of wrecks who inhabit Tony's: "At this, Langston fell away from the table in a violent spasm of trembling. 'It's okay,' he offered, making for his booth. 'An early one, it'll pass. But I don't think I should be near the breakables right now.'" Not since Huck Finn's father have I seen a character so willing lay out his planned DT's, but then Miles has another excuse, he's been blinded by an exploding aerosol can of grease cleaner during a shootout. Talk about blind drunk.

Osmond is obese, cowardly, and finishes himself by hiding and then consuming a full bottle of 151 rum. Miles is just an easily-agitated alcoholic, but one scene will do to render both. It is the morning the power is out, and everyone who drinks is getting up way still drunk and way hungover and trying to make something like sense out of this new day: "(Miles) wanted to panic but had grown accustomed to leaving that role to Osmond's Costello (as in Abbott & Costello) and then playing things a bit cooler....Osmond wanted out of this knowledge, all of it, just as Miles wanted out of Osmond at the moment."

Of course, the real *textual* issue here is that plot-wise, O'Brien seems to have gone full speed at painting himself into corners. Very few novels make so many promises in the first chapter, and I cannot imagine myself being alone in thinking on page 28, "Okay, O'Brien, let's see you explain all *this*."

Well, by God, he tried.

At this point, I'm going to press on and leave plot out of the observations and commentary. Technically, a sequence of events is a plot, and one expects the usual trimmings of conflict, character development, rising and falling action and all that, but by the third chapter, for me, anyway, it's not a matter of wondering what happens next so much as it is when will I read more lines with O'Brien hitting narrative grace notes that his characters don't deserve.

But for purists, here's the plot summary of *The Assault on Tony's*:

Drunks go to Tony's, get more drunk. With guns. Drunks trapped in Tony's by riot outside. Bartender shot. Free booze. Drunks shoot back. Drunks get drunker. Guns are compared. Drunks brave the streets outside to get more ammo, kill two *others*. Waitress fucks drunks and busboy. Weird liberal enters and soon leaves. Busboy fucks waitress *and* fat homophobe and leaves and gets shot. They run out of booze and die.

Or not. Just *you try* and run that for 288 pages and see if you can keep Aristotle, Derrida, the New Critics, Freud and your local schoolmarm in the Tuesday Night Book Club happy.

But back into the fray--or more fittingly, back into what's in this fray that makes it worth being back into. Without a lot of *schmaltz* about context or significance, let's just look at five sentences from various points in the novel:

> 1. "Oh, we're going all right," said Rudd from behind the bar. "Just as soon as you get sober, which should

be right after this drink."

2. Outside the night was still as fucking graffiti.

3. The hot dog rolled out of its bun and pleated-paper tray across half of Fenton's Lexus's roof, leaving mustard kisses at intervals of (approximately) pi H-M/2, where H represents the diameter of the hot dog and M the width of the mustard dollop.

4. Cash and Cards looked at this fat white fuck as if he were the best pork roast in the whole meat counter.

5. Fenton tossed back his share of the waning supply of J&B, not sure if he needed to want it or wanted to need it.

By no means are these examples a "best of" list from *Tony's*-- they're an almost random sample of lines I noted in my first read. But it's pretty clear that writers write such lines to show that writing is fun, and in some cases, it strikes a note of *joy* for the reader and probably for the writer as he wrote. THAT is the precious metal in the ore of this book, and there's a whole lot more in O'Brien's work. But it takes a reader some work to get at it, all right.

Thus, the somewhat predictable conundrum for the reader of *The Assault on Tony's* is that the *plot* part of the brain has lost interest by page 140, and the *character* part of the brain is losing interest fast now that the omniscient immersions into every player in the book have become the equivalent of a 90% done paint-by-numbers canvas, and in some other part of the reader's brain there seems to be an agent knocking at the door--something about rent being overdue for the Suspension of Disbelief Suite.

And yet just like the alcoholic takes comfort in knowing that the next sip of whiff of the *top-shelf stuff* will come, the reader, well, keeps going. And while that might mean that for the reader too far gone on O'Brien's distilled fine lines there comes a moment somewhere in Day 10--an oh shit moment, if you will--that the realization hits: *The stuff getting me high is going to run out. Oh shit!* So we're suddenly somehow like Rudd, Langston, Osmond, Miles and Fenton in a perverse way (for those of us who are alcoholics, sober or no, well, that's literal and *But for the grace of God* and all that--not a lot of Higher Power to ride with here). And the catharsis is thus doubly foreshadowed. It sucks when something that zaps the pleasure centers of the brain is about to be done. Of course, neither cirrhosis nor alcohol poisoning will see the reader off, unless that's part of some other plan. But no doubt about it, there is a weird and pleasant *delirium* in pressing on with this book; you don't need that tenth beer tonight, but it's going down just fine, thank you.

It's time we had a little date with Jill, the novel's most sympathetic, hygienic, necessary, complex, durable, self-doubting-yet-confident, and simultaneously the all-around most interesting. Also she has great tits.

The dialogue stream I imagine between myself at age 38 and Jill's I'd had I ended up in Tony's for a few beers goes something like this:

"You're a healthy, attractive woman, Jill. What do you do for fun?"

"Nothing."

"What do you do in your spare time?"

"Hate myself because it's a lighter lift than hating everyone else."

"Wanna go have some coffee somewhere after your shift?"

"No but we can go to my place and you can fuck me and leave, or maybe a blow job. Whatever."

Lots of O'Brien's central intelligent omniscience for Jill is like a multiplication problem, and the problem is $P \times Q \times Z \times Y \times 0 \times N =$. P,Q,Z,Y and N sure make you think, but in the end, the product is a kind of zero despite the thinking (two can play the math problem analogy, Mr. Smartypants O'Brien). And Jill is also the sort of woman whose wounded inner teenage Goth is inevitably going to stay inside and perpetually remain wounded. Outwardly, the depressed Goth bummer *riding high on a deep depression* (thx, Garbage) is not even close to an available *persona* for a 30-something in L.A. trying to eat and pay rent, so she gets into her fuckable waitress costume every day and works at Tony's--which is not to reduce Jill nor her real-life avatars to a non-human sex object. The dilemma for the reader and for the real women from whom a character like Jill springs is to either buy into the abject hope that some imperfect Mr. (or MS) Right is out there, wounded inner-Goth or not, and keep a smile on and cast pheromones about, or to accept being another rock on the landscape and just let erosion happen and hope the horizon is an attractive sunset. It sucks, and yet, unlike the hellbound drunks of this book, Jill does not let it consume her moment-by-moment and become the be-all and end-all.

To take my conversation with Jill to its conclusion:

"Why do you fuck so much so well for those you fuck while hating them and yourself while you're fucking them so well?"

"It's a kind of talent, I guess, that reminds me I really do exist sometimes. It all started happening around when, to other people, my tits and legs subordinated my eyes and voice."

It's easy to sort of identify what's wrong with Jill, but unlike her alcoholic colleagues (whose Fates are merely sped up), Jill's potential holds a much better set of outcomes. Better than she realizes. Jill is the only woman in the novel, but Jill is Everywoman, too. A little Gloria Steinem, a little Katy Perry, a little Mother Teresa, and more than a touch of Stormy Daniels. But unfortunately for Jill, the only exhibits in her Hall of Fame are bouncing on her ribcage.

Since John O'Brien isn't around to ask (and he'd be stupid to answer if he was), one asks what sort of writers and writing did he model as his craft evolved. And it's speculation, of course, but the evidence is available. The opening scenes evoke Hemingway's To Have and Have Not, the stream-of-consciousness has Faulkner-lite with a hint of Cleveland smart-ass, and some of the action scenes and descriptions point deliciously at Raymond Chandler. Having grown up in suburban Cleveland and being exposed to the canon of Great White American Male Voices in my own formative writing years (I'm 62; O'Brien would be 57 now), I'm dead-solid certain on Hemingway and Chandler. No doubt, Joseph Heller and Philip Roth got in the mix, and scents of Jay McInerney's Bright Lights, Big City float through some scenes.

But I don't mean to weigh down the reading of The Assault on Tony's by claiming it's a chowder of derivation. Think of it this way: Cars in 2018 are generally really efficient, safe, and dependable compared to cars in, say, 1970. And cars in 2018 also all look alike. If a blue Hyundai sped away from a crime scene at ten o'clock at night and I only got a glimpse, odds are they'd have to find a Honda/Toyota/Kia/Hyundai/Chevy/Ford/Subaru. By which I mean that writers consciously choose certain stylistic elements because they work, and they work via style to assemble the voice, and the voices are ultimately the steel and rubber and glass that make the thing we get into and drive when we read. O'Brien's ride is pretty damned nice here, even if ultimately the car doesn't go 200,000 miles worth of story.

The other thing invested readers may want to know of a novel like this is "Where in hell did the Genesis of this extreme plot come from?"

117

Fear not--I have a theory, and the short answer is: Cleveland. And of course, the 1992 L.A. riots on the heels of the Rodney King/L.A. Police verdict.

Baby-boomers from The Best Location in the Nation/Mistake on the Lake grew up in an era of upheaval and violence--largely on TV but also, in greater Cleveland, by word-of-mouth, and, in some cases, in person. Granted, O'Brien was born in 1960, so odds are he wouldn't have had a strong memory of, say, the JFK assassination (which I, born in 1955, do), but it's almost certain that between the Hough (1966), Glenville (1968), and Collinwood (1970) riots, some images and narrative probably trickled into the O'Brien household, as they did into mine.

And if you want to take a shot at explaining the alcohol-driven barricaded scenario, it's worth knowing that there were some bars in Cleveland where the barricading did take place. Hough, Glenville, and Collinwood were all neighborhoods whose racial tension came after an inertia of white flight, real estate gouging, and so on. But businesses like bars in those neighborhoods kept hold of the old white clientele because that's how drunks roll, and there is no doubt that white in those places armed themselves.

And while I never embraced the racist rants of the white-flighters who moved to my suburb (Willoughby), it's not that much of a stretch to see where the young O'Brien might have gotten his own dose of the kind of vitriol evidenced in the white patrons of Tony's from growing up in Brecksville or Lakewood.

They say that racism has to be learned by children and that it's not a natural thing, and I would agree. But to white children growing up in Cleveland suburbs in the 1960's and 70's, one had to be in a household where, once one entered school, the parents made a very conscious decision to not let the pervasive racism of other adults translate down a generation into those white kids. To wit, the day after Martin Luther King, Jr. was killed, I went to school and said something about how depressing it was.

"Fucking nigger-lover ," one of my classmates said to me.

So two things: 1. I'm giving credit to O'Brien for *using* the racism that's all-too-evident in America and not casting him in with his racist characters. (I'll nod to his sister Erin saying that if he, John O'Brien, cast himself into one of the characters in the novel, it would be the interloping liberal, Carey.) And 2. Armed insurrection in order to redistribute wealth and power might be the only way it'll ever happen in America--you can frame the Reagan or Trump or Clinton or Bush eras on this. Wealth has trickled up a ton in the past 70 years, and it's not like people are going to sit up from their dreams and say, "Hey, wait a minute! I should *share* more.

And anyone who thought the election of Barack Obama earmarked a *post-racial* America, please see the Disney production of *Oedipus Rex*.

The riot that fuels *The Assault on Tony's* is, when you think on it, one of the more easily-accepted aspects of the book. It's not a Cleveland story, but it's a story a kid from Cleveland might grow up to write. Especially an alcoholic kid from Cleveland.

Finally, we have to ask where to put this novel in our files under novel. Late 20th Century America, check. Hard-boiled narrative, check. Insightful omniscience, check. Humor, pulse, and *pathos* in the characters, double-check. The best American novel since sliced bread or beer in cans? No. A disturbing vision of a world in which such flawed men might behave exactly as the ones here? Yup.

Yet the perverse truth is that were it not for the screen success of *Leaving Las Vegas* and O'Brien's gunshot suicide in the mix, it's doubtful that this novel would have ever seen print in the 1990's. First off, well-rendered as Rudd, Miles, Osmond, Fenton, Langston, Jill and The Busboy are, they are not characters we enjoy projecting ourselves into. And while I can imagine myself in Tony's, it's not my first choice, mostly because there's so little *hope* in it.

I can only only imagine the conversation between O'Brien's agent (assuming he had one) and an editor I dealt with in the early 1990's:

"So what did you think, Gordon? Can this kid write or what?"

"He's got more talent in two pages than half the stable of Tom Clancy/Dan Brown shit-shovelers we print. But we can't market this. Who are we going to sell it to? Alcoholic writers from Cleveland? I love talent, but people want pablum."

Thank heaven for Grove Press.

'Nuff said. But if this novel has one redemption I can pitch, it's this--anyone who wants to write a novel with some pop should read John O'Brien if for nothing else other than the *exemplum* it is of putting flesh and blood into action with incredible and economic use of sentence, scene, and dialogue. He knew these people in his novel were not attractive or heroic and that his very plot premise and opening scene promised a shitshow. That's the fucking point. Most of us aren't. And our world is crazy, violent, and beyond our control. Especially for addicts. Until the Disney thing, of course.

Kelly Flamos discusses *The Assault On Tony's* with R.A. Washington

Kelly: When I read this book I had just read Leaving Las Vegas before I read this book. I also read many other books which explored addiction. I read Under The Volcano, The Lost Weekend, and this nonfiction book by Leslie Jamison that just came out this year called The Recovering in which she discusses drinking and writing.

R.A. Yes, I've heard of that.

Kelly: She wrote her Ph.D. at Yale with the topic of alcoholism and American Literature.

R.A. I hope she included O'Brien.

Kelly: She did not. However, my original thought about being a part of this project when Rob reached out to me was, since she didn't include O'Brien, I will fill in the gaps within and around her work. Rob asked me to be apart of Tony's* instead so here we are.

R.A. Well, I know first hand, through our many discussions over the years, that you talk about books very well. Plus I understand that Suzanne* recommended you to Rob so that just confirms it.

Kelly: So I'm reading this book and I'm done with it. And all I can think about is the alcohol and Jamison's book. There's this other plotline that's during the L.A. riots around the time of Rodney King and there's white guys and guns and those characters driving the story forward, but I think that for me what I got out of it was the way one can become trapped by an addiction, and the next drink was the obsession.

R.A. Yes and being trapped by the riot and truly not knowing where the eventual next drink would come if they stay trapped brilliantly magnifies the feeling of being trapped and obsessed by the alcohol.

Kelly: Arnold's Snyder wrote basically that the most interesting part of the novel has to do with the character's addiction to alcohol. Do you agree?

R.A. No, I don't agree. There's so much more to this story, these characters than just their addiction to alcohol. It just seems to me like maybe O'Brien found himself in situations where people really got fucked up. That was the circles he moved in. You see a group of people like that with addiction and alcohol and they could be some of the least interesting people you'd meet. Might be the most interesting but it wouldn't be because of the addiction. Some of these characters reminded me more of Frank from Shameless than characters you'd find in a Kerouac novel. I can see that made you laugh.

I think it's an oversimplification to say he used any of that as a trope for instance. I'm not saying that addiction and alcoholism aren't explored, even in the forefront often. He's talking, exploring, examining other themes just as, probably more important, continually reminding you of the class of the people, workers, country club members, he's talking about class, race, society. So do I agree that the most interesting part of this novel has to do with the characters' addiction? No, no I do not agree.

Kelly: I dig it. I see where you're going with that...Another part, I guess, that is challenging for me is...this is supposed to be fiction and I'm having a problem separating everything I read about the author from the work but I've been assured that many people who are involved in talks from the other books have felt the same way.

R.A. I think about the author too but in a different way. I just imagine him after the Rodney King riots and so forth just sitting in a bar and listening to these privileged jerks and just then his wheels just started turning right, and then he writes a page and then he writes the second page and so on. Yeah, that's how I imagine it.

Kelly: OK, Rafeeq, so you read this book a couple of years ago, preparing for contributing to this book, the project had some delays and so you read it again for our conversation this evening?.

R.A. Yep, that's correct.

Kelly: Anything change since then that may give you another perception or an additional one!??? Make it more or at least relevant in a different way???

R.A. More specifically, haha, you are asking about reading it before and after 2016. I'll take that as rhetorical.

Kelly: Mostly, but what changed this time around.

R.A. Well, other than the obvious which you are alluding to, yes, of course, these guys are still around, many thought they were gone, I never did. Maybe went into hiding but they haven't gone anywhere. On another, non-political note, I think this book may have been closer to being done than before. The first time I read it I assumed it was the first draft but reading it through this time, I think he may have put more work into it, gotten further than I originally thought. Or, maybe I just picked up more with a second reading, which shouldn't be surprising.

Kelly: It has changed in more than one way than with a second reading.

R.A. If this is actually the first draft? The sentence and some of the paragraph construction indicate that it isn't. Has it come out that way the first time through? It's too pristine for me to think that there wasn't more work put into it. I can't remember why I thought a few years ago that it was a first or at least an early draft. Too well done to be accidental…and the things that he appears to make mistakes on, you know, the MFA grad type of mistakes, you know, novel 101 type stuff, the rules, all of the damn rules, there's moments in the dialogues, some of the tongue-in-cheek moments, where I feel he was manipulating rules, not that he didn't know them, he may have even been making fun of them. I'm not saying that it was finished by any stretch, I'm not saying there wasn't work to be done or that if he would have had a chance to work with a good editor that there wouldn't be a benefit. There are some plot-device issues, maybe he thought it would make the book more sellable? Easily fixable, can't imagine they wouldn't have been fixed. But the first draft? Naw.

If I may take a detour, if you remember around the Rodney King verdict there was a nice contingent of American society and it got louder and louder, represented by most of the dudes in this book. We were saying, thinking Shut The Fuck Up! We don't want to hear anything from you. O'Brien nails that vibe…I found those feelings from 30 or so years ago welling up again. But O'Brien isn't going to make it that easy for me, is he? These characters are too rounded just to hate. He actually, and it's not easy to achieve, makes them somewhat sympathetic. " I'm disenfranchised in a whole other way.

I might not be able to have a better life. Life, this might be as good as it gets." You are soaked in despair.

It's not necessarily like he's telling you a verbatim story from his life. But it's colored with the despair. I think older writers could relate to what I'm trying to express. He's a writer's writer. That's why I would have loved the opportunity to talk with some of the literary conventions he was attempting here. He may have been what, at most, in his early '30s when he wrote this books. Feels like someone in at least their '50s, again I think there are some older writers who would understand what I mean.

Kelly: How old were you when you wrote Citi?

R.A. Thirty-eight, thirty-nine. I tried to write Citi well before that. I couldn't have written it in my early '30s no matter how badly I wanted to. I wasn't ready. I wrote a novel called Open but it was too early for me to be trying some of the things that I initially tried. I eventually figured it out.

It took me longer than it should have because of what my thoughts about what maleness was and should be. Just that outlook effects intensely everything from culture to internal thoughts, internal life. I wanted to write soulfully and I had to contend, overcome that, or at least attempt to. Since the canon exists of mostly men so the signals that I received is that a good novel had certain parameters. Listen, like Bukowski and Fante, O'Brien has his share of misogyny. But for me, again like Bukowski and Fante, he's honest about it. There's an honesty to it.

Kelly: And the existence of it is unfortunate but it does exist and, to act like it doesn't is disingenuous.

R.A. And it all needs to come out. It all needs to be laid bare. And character is the writer's way to show it. We need it all. Beckett, Toni Morrison, want to see some misogynistic characters? It all has to be there. Ivanhoe to Brooks. The ability to play within the entirety of Western Civilization? Borges does that.

Now, with contemporary writers, like the John O'Briens of the world, I'm not sure we have a frame, or even a lexicon, on how to critique them. We may be right in the middle of trying to figure all of that out and it may take quite a bit of hindsight. To understand how to be critical.

Kelly: I'm trying to see if I follow you, with Toni Morrison for example, or any of these writers, O'Brien being, for the sake of this discussion at least, the stand-in for contemporary writers, they have to be viewed not only as a part but as a whole? Western literature or Western civilization? Or there is a link?

R.A. Not necessarily like Toni Morrison read Zora Neale Hurston directly or I read O'Brien. Here's an example, once writers break enough social norms, clear enough land, Hunter S. Thompson, for example, makes it so that when I write I can write within that landscape and not even be thought of as on the forefront of anything. I think that's a good thing. So, maybe, and this may be a bit of a confused, roundabout way of stating it, though they are way more different than alike, Fante may have cleared a path for someone like O'Brien, including dealing with misogyny. And there's dozens and dozens of the same thing with racism, class and so on.

I can't know what was inside the head of John O'Brien let alone his heart as far as misogyny or any other trait is concerned. I can guess. I think he is Casey, the one character in the book without any of the ugly traits surrounding the Rodney King situation. Maybe I'm just wishing that since I admire the writing that I hope that IF he made one of the characters like him, it's not one of the right-wingers.

Kelly: Yeah, I agree, because the current situation, has kind of... made it OK for people to be...part of all of the "bad-isms." Acceptable in public even.

For me when I think about race in America I try to take this stance as a white woman that I have to have humility and I have to always remember that no matter what I've read or the people I know I do not know and I can't think that I know I have to keep learning and I do. And I keep I've read so many history books just this year and I am continually learning things that I didn't know about American history. I have no idea what it's like to be black in America. And I never will but I can keep learning and trying to understand through listening and trying to educate myself the best I can.

I don't know. At first, I found myself becoming annoyed that the riots were the backdrop and he didn't even try to delve into that more but I guess he's just trying to paint a picture of this working-class bar life and it wasn't really trying to be didactic? I think he felt that it was better not to lean too heavily. Not be too obvious and let the characters speak for themselves without losing how real they were and not just be a mouthpiece for a certain type. It would have been a mistake to write these characters as blatantly ignorant. Some have even begun to cherish ignorance. Now, there's even pride to it. Doesn't matter what the facts are, this stance, though misinformed, has a higher purpose than the truth.

Kelly: What are your thoughts on O'Brien beginning the novel at or toward the end?

R.A. It's a technique. It's probably more common in movies but there are plenty of books, especially in the 20th Century that employ the device. It removes the classic climax of the book. It's the author's intention not to surprise or make the value of the book an unexpected turn. This is what happens, now let's examine how the hell we got to this place. I think in some cases, and this is one of them, it places more weight on the bulk of the story.

There are formal concerns. The form of the novel. And then there's the storytelling in the novel. And the formal concerns. Subjectively we often don't remember things in linear time anyway. In the end, I just think it was a choice he made formally on what he most wanted to emphasize.

Kelly: Another thought I had when I was reading is why do riots, especially sudden riots happen? Why people revolt almost simultaneously? So, these guys hole up in a bar, and it gives them, at least a sense, of control. Others outside revolting have much less control of their situation. Here's the thing though: they are rioting because of systems that have destabilized any control they have over their lives.

So the men inside the bar have more control in normal circumstances AND during a riot, even though they have no control over their addictions. Their privilege still gives them more control or power. I may be mistaken, but I don't think there is even a real discussion about why there is a riot. They don't seem to even care about the whys, which to me strips the dignity of the rioters substantially more than if they were virulently against the cause of the rioters, even to the point of overt bigotry. At least try to understand even if you come out on the other side. It's the indifference that's chilling. I hope he meant to do that because it's effective.

Anyway, One of the many things that Patrick Snee brought up in his essay about Tony's is that perhaps O'Brien was using L.A. in the early '90s as a metaphor or maybe analogy would be the better word and he's really speaking to the riots that occurred in Cleveland in the late '60s and early '70s. This is fascinating and added a whole new layer for me. I think it's worth quoting it here for context: "The other thing invested readers may want to know of a novel like this is "Where in hell did the Genesis of this extreme plot come from?" Fear not--I have a theory, and the short answer is: Cleveland. And of course, the 1992 L.A. riots on the heels of the Rodney King/L.A. Police verdict.

Baby-boomers from The Best Location in the Nation/Mistake on the Lake grew up in an era of upheaval and violence--largely on TV but also, in greater Cleveland, by word-of-mouth, and, in some cases, in person. Granted, O'Brien was born in 1960, so odds are he wouldn't have had a strong memory of, say, the JFK assassination (which I, born in 1955, do), but it's almost certain that between the Hough (1966), Glenville (1968), and Collinwood (1970) riots, some images and narrative probably trickled into the O'Brien household, as they did into mine. And if you want to take a shot at explaining the alcohol-driven barricaded scenario, it's worth knowing that there were some bars in Cleveland where the barricading did take place. Hough, Glenville, and Collinwood were all neighborhoods whose racial tension came after an inertia of white flight, real estate gouging, and so on. But businesses like bars in those neighborhoods kept hold of the old white clientele because that's how drunks roll, and there is no doubt that white in those places armed themselves."

R.A. Yeah. I mean, If you're from Cleveland and of a certain age the riots are an integral part of this city. Even if you don't know anything about them or you weren't there, the riots are a part of this city. It informs how you, the history of the riots, even the movement of the city, whether you like it or not.

If Cleveland and not L.A. is the true genesis of this book well let's discuss this because if that is true then it's relevant to this book. The Hough riots started because it was a disagreement between some officers and a man named Evans who ran a black watch type organization. It escalated from there to the Glenville riot which arose from the situation of the mayor using street gangs to police certain areas in addition to the corruption in city government and the police department trying to frame certain individuals. They brought in the National Guard and they brought in Elliot Ness who nabbed Capone in his earlier years. Ness was given the orders to break up the Glenville riot.

Kelly: I've been reading so much history lately but I hadn't come across that. I just read These Truths by Jill Lepore and she talks about how many American slaves gained their freedom by fighting for the British and now by reading a novel by John O'Brien and being apart of this discussion I find there is much more recent history right here that I need to read about.

We are running out of time but I wanted to make sure we at least touched on this. I want to end on going back to the Snee essay which will be in this book too and get your thoughts on this part, Rafeeq. Again, I'm going to read the entire passage because I'm curious what you can add or what comes to mind.

"The other part of thing two sorts out pretty well. The Assault on Tony's is not so much plot driven as it's situationally compacted and by virtue of the cage setting the extremity of the characters gets a hefty shove into being what the story is about. And in the constraints,

O'Brien has built for himself in this novel he uses his gymnastic abilities with omniscience scene and language on the sentence level to well kind of show off. And it's rather enjoyable watching him hot dog on the page especially as he performs tricks that seem almost preposterous in their concept but somehow find paydirt as we read on one can what if a lot of stuff about this book. But it's never in doubt that this is one gifted son of a bitch at the helm."

Thoughts?.

R.A. Yeah, I mean of course and I agree. I agree with Snee. The ways in which some of the characters are constructed and the ways in which he avoids plot at times and just lingers with these characters.

Again, that's why I think he puts the ending at the beginning, at least part of the reason. In fact, it's spot on and I really don't think anything I can say will elaborate or enhance it. When this book comes out Snee's essay is the first part I'm going to read. Good stuff.

Kelly: I've liked hearing you talk about this Rafeeq because you're a novelist and that gives me new perspectives. It deepens my appreciation for O'Brien. One thing that I can't stop thinking about was your earlier comment about when you were asked about writing your novel Citi and how you tried in your early 30s, again, about the time O'Brien wrote his novels, and you weren't ready and how maleness and misogyny played a factor.

And one of my big hang-ups is when I met you and we talked about books and I started reading O'Brien and it made me take a turn because I was reading all of these women writers, some in translation, and this was so far from where I wanted to be. Oh man, I have this awesome thing going with reading all of these awesome women and, initially, this guy is not my scene. Also, because he's from Cleveland his personal story can overshadow and I have a problem separating the author from the work and initially I found that frustrating.

The maleness that kind of stunted you I eventually found in this work something profound. I'm a mother and I have boys and instead of having my first instinct to criticize it I found myself more and more wanting to understand it. In this novel, and we haven't discussed this much with the limited time we have but the character Jill. No woman wants to relate to that but maybe that's how guys, at least some, relate. And after the sense of revulsion of the idea something brutally real is relayed?

R.A.:Certainly one of my favorite male Cleveland writers and he handles the muck as well as anyone.

Kelly: He's up there I take it. What other male writers, from Cleveland, do you recommend, other than yourself of course.

R.A. The Decapites, both father and son, O'Brien of course, Megenhardt, Chessnut. Off the top of my head, those are five Cleveland male novelists I dig. Plenty of women too but that's for another day I guess.

Kelly: Thanks for Sharing

R.A.: I am honored to take part in this.

Stripper Lessons

Salvation at the Strip Club

Sara Dobie Bauer

I meet Gia for coffee at a boisterous Cleveland coffee shop on a freezing Sunday afternoon during Browns season, surrounded by hung-over business professionals, hipster bartenders, and, well, at least one stripper.

Gia and I first made eye contact a million years ago at Larry Flynt's Hustler Club on Center Street. My husband actually pointed her out during one of her dances. Beneath the shuddering green-blue-red lights, he said, "Jesus, look at that one." I remember she didn't move like the other girls; she was *more*. An ex-gymnast, training for the circus (which I didn't even know was a thing anymore), she did graceful handstands to the beat of heavy metal while other girls gyrated on a greased pole. My husband bought me a lap dance—oh, the perks of having a bisexual wife—and although Gia's muscular body did keep my attention, we ended up talking about books, and I eventually got her number.

Over coffee, I tell her about John O'Brien, this Cleveland author who moved to LA before committing suicide because—in the words of his sister—he "wanted to get as far away from Cleveland as he could." I tell Gia about *Stripper Lessons*, about the protagonist Carroll and his relationship to the fictional strip club Indiscretions. Carroll has to be there every night and feels a desperate panic at the thought of missing out.

As if this is old news, and maybe it is, Gia says, "Oh, I had one of those." She sips her coffee. No matter she was up dancing until 4 AM, she's glowing, rested, probably because she's not much of a drinker and she certainly doesn't do drugs. In her free time, she goes to New York City and practices handstands with actual circus professionals. You can't make this shit up.

I press her for more.

"Yep." She nods. "There was this guy at Hustler who used to come in every single night from 7 PM to 2:30 AM. He sat in the same booth, he ordered the same dinner, and he talked to the same girls. Everyone knew him. He seemed harmless, so I started talking to him. I even gave him my number. For, I don't know, a year, we even talked on the phone for hours at a time. I found myself growing attracted to him. During lap dances, I would let him finger me."

A no-no at strip clubs, in case you were wondering.

Gia tucks her short, brown bob behind her ears and owns that crowded coffee shop. She's alluring like a mythical creature, a mermaid, a siren...I'm pretty sure she could kick my ass. She continues, "I saw him for two years. We had this really intimate emotional relationship. Anyway, after all that talking on the phone and special treatment at the club, I heard some other girl call him 'Henry.' I was like, 'Who's Henry?'" Here, she leans forward, about to divulge all the secrets of the universe. "He never even gave me his real name, Sara," she says. "As soon as I found out, I never talked to him again. It'd been fake the whole time, everything I thought we had. Can you fucking believe that?"

* * *

I meet Cleveland author Rob Jackson for coffee on the tree-covered back porch of his house in Mentor, outside the city. Despite the dying orange-red leaves, it's an unseasonably warm day that almost makes you forget winter is coming and tends to stay forever like a pair of claws in your shoulders that you eventually ignore because, at some point, you're used to the pain.

Rob asks if I've ever heard of some writer guy, John O'Brien—a Cleveland author apparently, who wrote *Leaving Las Vegas*. ("Of course, you've heard of *Leaving Las Vegas*.") I have heard of the movie but don't have the heart to tell Rob I've never seen it because, by now, his eyes glitter with a desperate hope I have yet to understand because I have yet to "meet" John.

Rob explains he's getting a bunch of Cleveland authors together to read John's work and respond to it. He hands me a book called *Stripper Lessons*, and I make a joke. "Strippers, huh? Did the blue hair and nose piercing give me away?" That or maybe the way I dress way sluttier than other thirty-six-year-old women I know.

Rob only looks flustered for a second before he remembers it's *me*—that I'm joking. Then, he smiles because he knows the only way he's going to offend me is by talking about book censorship or Ohio State football.

The front cover of *Stripper Lessons* is black and simple with a tiny circular picture of a naked woman. The back cover says nothing about the book's contents, just showers praise on *Leaving Las Vegas* and a book I've never heard of, *The Assault on Tony's*.

Rob asks me to read it—"Just read it, and tell me what you think." Then, I have to decide if I want to spend my time penning an essay about this dead guy who, over coffee on Rob's back porch, means nothing to me. But I trust Rob now and have since I met him at a poetry open mic in Painesville two years prior. He's good-looking in that young 1980s Don Henley way with the perpetual ponytail and bad boy enthusiasm.

I take the book home and start reading. By page two, I realize John O'Brien reminds me a lot of Chuck Palahniuk without the massive ego that bleeds down pages of his books until your hands are covered in the sticky residue of arrogance. There's no arrogance here, not in *Stripper Lessons*. There's a sad, invisible man named Carroll—basically Mister Cellophane from *Chicago*. People don't see him; they walk right by. He's scared of things like a jiggling light fixture and his co-worker's spaghetti. He's in a never-ending search for a missing file at the office, the dreaded SoLo/Bombgate. But then, every night, there is peace.

Indiscretions, the strip club, feels like home. ("More of a place-he-likes-to-be than anywhere else he's ever been.") He'll be there every night. ("Not that there's ever any question of not coming.")Carroll knows the routine. He drinks his sparkling apple cider and watches all the girls do one-two-three dances until, one night, an angel descends from Heaven in the form of Stevie. He sees it as a sin not to look at her. It's blasphemous to think her anything less than divine. Silently, he begs, "Save me."

* * *

I have coffee with John's sister, Erin O'Brien. When I sit across from her in the Chesterland coffee shop, I feel like I've met her before. Maybe it's the Cleveland accent or the way she pulls at her long black-grey hair and calls it "witch hair." We're surrounded by Halloween decorations: paper cutouts of pumpkins, pumpkin candles, and even pumpkin-flavored coffee.

There's no way to ask a woman if her dead brother frequented strip clubs, so of course, I ask the woman if her dead brother frequented strip clubs.

She smiles and leans back in her seat—not offended but amused. "I wonder how many strip clubs he went to under the name of research." We share a laugh. "But the sparkling apple cider, three sets, the table dances—he knew those details—so he had the details nailed."

But, really, tell me about John.

In *Stripper Lessons*, Carroll is the invisible man. Women think he's harmless and kind of cute, but he's a loser. He's walked all over. John O'Brien took his own life in 1994 at the age of thirty-three after years spent fighting alcoholism and its ever-present sidekick depression. I've seen pictures of John in his leather jackets with his swoopy dark hair and see nothing of Carroll.

Erin sets me straight. "I think John was evoking his teenage self with Carroll. This is *Johnny*, not sullied by liquor. It's the Johnny that I miss so very much, the Johnny that doesn't have all this darkness."

As a young man, Erin says John was awkward and yet smooth. She believes the booze acted as a bridge between the two. She says he would have charmed me. He would have hit on me, tried to make me laugh. He would have twitched his wrist, not in a cocky attention grab for his prized possession—his Rolex—but because that was how the watch was wound, by moving his wrist.

We're having such a nice time, Erin and I. She fawns over my weird hair, and I go way off topic to talk about her podcast and famous Cleveland cemeteries. The pumpkin spice decaf is excellent, so why do I have to go and ruin things by talking about addiction?

"John was addicted to alcohol," I say. "Carroll is addicted to the strip club. Do you think that was intentional, like a way to work out his own demons?"

Erin seems hesitant, because even though she's John's sister, she doesn't want to put words in his mouth. "I don't know his intention. He was trying so hard on the religious themes ..."

True statement. *Stripper Lessons* is rife with them. Stevie is an angel descended from Heaven. On his way to a wedding, Carroll gets lost and ends up at a church. He seeks that missing Solo/Bombgate file as he seeks Stevie's approval and attention—as a pilgrim seeks Mecca. Carroll wants to believe in a higher power ("You just gotta *believe* in something"), which is possibly why I'm shocked when Erin tells me John was an adamant atheist.

I make a joke about how most of my most angry atheist friends just want to go to church. Maybe I'm not too far off base with John, but again, let's not go putting words in a dead guy's mouth.

* * *

Driving home from coffee with Erin, I feel a heavy sadness

that's like an iceberg in my chest. My father calls. We talk about my brother—coincidentally, a recovering addict and atheist—and how my writing is going. I'm only halfway listening, still back at that Chesterland coffee shop, still reliving the way Erin's strong, confident voice didn't shake.

"When he would be in the throes of DTs, he would always see devils coming through the walls. He once recounted a story to our mother: during the last moments before he surfaced from the live-action nightmare, everything stopped at once. Then an angelic female voice pierced the blackness, crystalline and sweet. 'We've lost you,' she said, 'but we'll get you back.' When his brain was frying out in DTs, what'd he see? What was John's deepest fear? The devil coming at him. What the hell happened to him? Is he burning in hell, or is he singing with angels? Or is he just gone?"

* * *

I have coffee with Gia and find out she's been stripping since she was nineteen, now twenty-seven. During the short months when she actually dates, she stops stripping, takes a break. She doesn't tell her boyfriends she strips. She's been broken up with before for even mentioning stripping in her past.

Who would break up with this goddess? Who could look at her on that green-blue-red stage at Hustler and feel anything but divinity in the room? Listen to me, waxing poetic, but I swear her skin glows. She's all muscle and soft places (in the *right* places), and I have no idea how tall she is because she always wears heels and so do I. For years, people have assumed I'm ridiculously tall, but it's all a lie. Another façade, like my blue hair that covers layers of white.

"Do you think men are addicted to strip clubs?" I ask.

Gia is too sweet to look at me like I'm an idiot, but her athletic posture weaves like a drunk guy walking the line. "It's totally an addiction. Just like money to a stripper, it's a dependency issue. It's a high in a different way." She pauses and picks at a gluten-free muffin. "It's so twisted, though. Who goes to a strip club every night? What kind of person is that? All of our fetishes are so crazy, our addictions. The things that drive us."

* * *

Next time I have coffee with Rob, he's worried I might think *Stripper Lessons* is sexist, which is silly once you get used to Carroll's voice. The man doesn't know how to be sexist.

("After all, what does he know about sex?")

Stripper Lessons isn't pornographic. It's barely sexual at all.

It's about church, in a way, a man addicted to worship. Even Stevie's shaved pussy gets "reverential treatment." Carroll's new clothes are a "small offering." I think Erin O'Brien says it best: "This is a book about getting and losing your religion."

Carroll is seeking, seeking, searching for something at Indiscretions (just like that damn file at work), and he finds that something when Stevie walks on stage, this angel of a woman, this goddess that is—for some inexplicable reason—different from all the others. He has found his meaning in her existence; he has found his salvation. Like a religious zealot, he goes to "church" every night to worship at her feet, literally, since she's above him on stage. His addiction to the strip club becomes an addiction to one woman, and she is supposed to save him.

John was addicted to alcohol, but did he want to be saved? Does Carroll?

I worked with drug addicts three years ago and only lasted six months before I walked away for fear of becoming a jaded, hateful bitch of a person. I couldn't watch the clean, clear hope followed by

140

the drugged-up relapse. I couldn't hear the professions of "I want to get better," followed days later by an overdose ER visit. Frankly, I feared the permanent loss of sympathy as I watched addicts of all ages boomerang over and over. For a moment, I stopped believing in redemption.

An addict will not get better, will not get clean, unless they want to get clean. Parents can't force successful rehab on their kids. Friends can't get friends to put the needle down. Getting clean is up to the addict and the addict alone, and no matter how much Carroll thinks he wants Stevie to save him, the ending of *Stripper Lessons* paints the portrait of an addict already looking for his next fix.

I try to be an optimist, so when Stevie agrees to coffee and fries at the diner with Carroll, I like to pretend their date happened. They became friends. They had a million babies. It's all bull shit.

As soon as Carroll realizes Stevie is actually *Jenny*, he sees the proverbial man behind the curtain.

Over coffee, Erin flails a little over this topic. Her calm composure leaves for but a moment. Her shoulders rise as though spoiling for a fight while she adjusts her glasses and stares at me. "At the end of the book when she's standing right in front of him, she is accessible, she is no longer on the stage, she is no longer the ethereal angel. She's just a regular woman. *Jenny* is her name." She says it with disdain. "When Carroll hears the name Jenny, he almost wishes that he wouldn't. When she steps off the stage, she becomes a real fleshed-out woman to him. It's like whoever was playing Mary in the school Christmas play goes outside and you see her smoking a cigarette. She's real, and Carroll doesn't want the real woman."

Carroll doesn't want to be saved.

Two weeks after signing the contract for the *Leaving Las Vegas* film (which would go on to Academy Award fame), John O'Brien shot himself.

Erin says, "I don't think it mattered at that point. It was too late;

he'd made his decision."

Did John escape addiction at the end? Was he destroyed or saved?

* * *

Only once, Carroll touches God. He touches Stevie, and it kills him. The next night, he's upset and makes a mistake that gets him banned from Indiscretions forever. He later pukes in an alley—an addict going cold turkey facing withdrawals. But his eyes are opened.

("Carroll is suddenly not so sure he ever belonged in a place like this … this is the first time he has ever regretted coming to this place.")

He realizes Stevie is not his salvation.

("She can't help him. She can't help her. She's not God.")

As a reader, do we feel relief at this point? Are we happy to see him free of his addiction or saddened at his loss of faith? Did he ever really want to be saved at all? You have to think no, because when Stevie… Jenny…finally offers herself, Carroll wonders if she is really what he's been looking for.

Do you want to be clean, Carroll? Do you want the day-to-day of your addiction to finally cease? Can this woman fix you, or is she just another bit of emptiness in your stupid, little life, just like that damned SoLo/Bombgate file: empty, nothing inside, just a shell that looks nice?

John himself was married for thirteen years to a woman his sister said "would have walked through fire for him." Once John filed for divorce, Erin knew he wouldn't last six months. He killed himself within a year, two weeks after signing a contract that maybe could have changed his life—but it was too late for him to be saved, if he wanted to be saved at all.

Johnny saw his angels and his demons. I bet they each offered a hand on his final day.

* * *

Over coffee with Erin, I read a line out loud from *Stripper Lessons*, a silly line about Ohio that made me laugh. She says, "I miss him so much."

It takes me a second to realize she's crying. Then, I start crying. Two grown ass women are crying in a Chesterland coffee shop while "The Monster Mash" plays in the background. We grab for napkins and dab our makeup.

Erin mumbles like she doesn't know she's doing it, like maybe she's talking to a ghost. "Oh, I miss that guy. I miss that guy. I'm not crying; you're crying. I never hear anybody read his stuff. I don't think I've ever heard anybody pick up one of his books and read it. Shit. Oh, Christ ..." Once we've calmed down enough to laugh, she says, "If anyone asks, you started crying first."

I never have coffee with John.

Stripper Lessons Roundtable

Sara Dobie Bauer
Christie Danzey
Marina Vladova

Sara: I thought we could all kind of just one at a time go through and say our general feelings about the book. So would you want to start?

I can start if you want. I didn't pick this book. I don't know about you guys. Rob actually gave it to me and suggested I read this one of all of John's work. I kind of picked on him and said, "Why? Because I look like a stripper?" But I was in love with this book from Page 5. I just really like the writing style. I really liked the naive innocence of Carroll, and I related to him on a lot of levels just because I have a lot of anxiety issues, and some of the anxieties that he had as a character, I really related to. Especially with the ceiling fan when was shaking and he was really paranoid and just the nervousness.

When he thought "I can't have the maintenance guy back again. He's been here once and it was awkward. And so now it's gonna be awkward forever" and that's how I think sometimes too. So I really I related to Carroll those ways but then I just enjoyed his journey. A lot of John's books are really heavy and sad, I enjoyed that this one didn't make me sad. I actually left this book feeling kind of hopeful. So I guess those are my generalized feelings on the book. That's how I felt.

Marina: I love the camaraderie, but I think we'll have divergent views, so that makes me look forward to the conversation. I love George Saunders's mantra of respecting the reader, and though what we've

144

read might be a draft version of *Stripper Lessons,* I felt at times not respected as a reader. I do find Carroll sympathetic—absolutely. But I find some of the writing hackneyed.

But there are moments, like describing the unbearably mechanical way an office operates, that are sublime. If the storyteller narrates Carroll's perspective, then we see a wry observer of the hierarchy— the "torpid partners" —and the energy—the "going-for-it-ness" —at a law firm. So, when I first began reading this, I did think it was self-indulgent in the way that *Metamorphosis* might have been. So I'm thinking OK. Kafkaesque, and then I actually see him at a point when Carroll's narratorial voice is talking about work, saying, "[I] was an insect to them". And I don't know if it is deliberate because so much of the writing is, as mentioned, hackneyed.

There are tendencies that remain unrecognized or undeveloped by the writer. Things, patterns O'Brien might not have been aware of. Cannibalistic elements, for example—the cuticles, licking perspiration, the blood. At one point while Carroll is home mirroring a stripper, I'm thinking that the story might take a *Silence of the Lamb*s homoerotic direction...thinking that Carroll wants to be a stripper or is experiencing gender dysphoria. But this doesn't happen.

Sara: Thank God!

Marina: There also are pedophilic moments—he so adores "angels" with no pubic hair. But I guess drafts are supposed to be self-indulgent because then you chisel...

Sara: Just so you know, according to John's sister, this isn't a draft. He was querying this already. He was sending this out to agents and publishers. So it was actually in his mind complete.*

It was done as far as he thought it was going to be finished. Erin is John's sister. She did the preliminary edit for it, but this is what we have that John wrote. He was actively trying to sell this to a publisher at the time of his death. So in his mind, this was complete, although it has a lot of draft like qualities that an editor probably would have changed.

Marina: Hmm. There seems to be a tonal shift or mimetic mode at the end that bookends with the qualifying phrase, "Dark, but not really". Maybe it's a moment of lighthearted enlightenment..."Seen enough?"

Sara: I share the opinion that it does not have a happy ending, thinking that once Jennifer becomes a real person, he never sees her again. And they never have a romance so they never meet at the coffee shop.

Marina: I'm wondering if even before she becomes Jennifer that this is all the fantasy of a sick or dying man and this last part or meeting Jennifer in a coffee shop doesn't even happen.

Sara: Christie, why don't you give us your take on it? The novel as a whole.

Christie: I haven't read a book like this in quite some time. I was taken in by it immediately, but it took me a little bit to get used to the writing style. At first, I had to read every paragraph twice to completely grasp what the writer was saying. However, as I read further and got used to John's writing style I didn't have to do that anymore. I thought it was fascinating. The way it was put together was mind-boggling. It's written in such a way that I could never comprehend writing something like this. I really enjoyed the writing style and some of the challenges that went along with reading it.

As far as the book itself and the character of Carroll I felt that he was very obviously delusional. I read the book once, and then I started a second reading of the book. Although I didn't complete the second reading, I was seeing things through a different lens than I did the first time. I think it's because I knew what was going to happen and I was familiar with the way it was written. The first time I read it, I think I was a little bit more sympathetic to Carroll, but the second time around I was really seeing him as a whole lot more delusional. I didn't feel like there really was a transformation in the character of Carroll as I first believed. From the first reading, I felt that he had a bit of self-reckoning, a coming into himself, and finding his boldness. However, my opinion changed with the second reading and what I saw was self-destruction. What I took from the second reading was that he was so delusional that he was out of control.

Marina: Stripper clubs are illusory.

Christie: It was like an unleashing of a different side of himself which was snowballing completely out of control. He ended up going from one extreme to another. He initially appeared to be shy and introverted. He had repressed so much and bottled it up inside and then all of a sudden he opened the floodgates. All that anxiety, that repression, everything he was holding back including his fear, just erupted. He didn't have the ability to self-regulate the things that he was saying and doing. Therefore I didn't see it as a transformation after all; instead, I saw it as a second negative side coming out.

I think at the end I was expecting a total annihilation. So I think that what happened to him at work did turn out the way that I expected it to. He left under duress and he obviously wasn't going to go back. He leaves his future so uncertain. He just maxed out his credit cards on all of those purchases for clothes and now he's not going to have any way to pay them off. Additionally, I was doing the mental math of how much money he must be spending at the strip club each night. The entrance fee to the club is eight dollars a night, each drink is $3.50 and it sometimes sounded like he was drinking five, six, seven drinks a night, and then add whatever money is he is putting down in tips. Even if you exclude the topless dances because those were an exceptional occurrence towards the end, he had to be spending $30-40 a night. On a File Clerk's salary that is quite a bit of regular spending. He is going to have a hard time finding another job between walking out on the law firm and his personality issues. So from the job standpoint, he had the self-destruction that I was expecting.

However, in the case of Jennifer, it did not go the way I was expecting. It is interesting to hear what you said, Marina, about the ending with Jennifer because to me it did feel a little bit hopeful at first but I was also confused. I wondered why she would be willing to connect with him outside of the club. I was trying to read into the character of Jennifer too.

Marina: So I don't think that happens with Jennifer. Here's what I think is real for Carroll—the scene described on page 188...top of the page..."Picking up the whiskey [...] he keeps it down [because he's a pro!]. Now puke just puke. I wonder, do we know?... Do we know that all along Carroll's been struggling not to drink? Or is it something that's just not ever really discussed?

Christie: I'm pretty sure that the book said he never drank, ever.

Marina: I think this whole dimly lit "trip" is about him trying not to resume drinking. And I think that it's when he interacts with the bartender and later when he pukes by the "Dumpster" where the writing becomes more authentic. He knows what he's talking about here. And when he starts drinking deliberately...it's the only time when I feel that the character and the narration is truly successful.. Otherwise, the novel is list-y with what seems like a series of asides instead of internal monologue.

Sara: Yeah, I guess but I feel like the whole book is about addiction because he's addicted to a strip club. That's something I've thought about with *Leaving Las Vegas*, which is arguably very autobiographical for John. It's about an alcoholic who dies eventually from alcoholism. This one, it almost felt like he was trying so hard not to talk about addiction, that he talked about addiction the whole time.

Marina: But I felt like he didn't know what he was addicted to-- before. You know it at first. I don't think that sequence at the end with "Jennifer" ever happens. That's where the tragedy is—you know, that he just can't connect. He doesn't connect, and he starts drinking again.

Sara: One of the questions is "Arnold Snider wrote, 'By refusing to divulge any biographical details about such a character, O'Brien makes Stripper Lessons a study of loneliness itself.' Agree or disagree?" And we can talk about the study of loneliness. But, I guess I want to talk about how Caroll has no backstory to us. He just like exists in this place but we don't know how he got there, why he's there, or why the strip club thing started happening.

Marina: Or if he drank before?

Sara: For my commentary on that, I feel like this book is almost like a capsule, where Caroll begins on page one and ends at the end. As Christie was talking about, he's lost his job but he's also lost Indiscretions (the name of the strip club) so he's lost all the things in his life that matter. So I almost feel like he appeared in scene one, and now he disappears from the universe at the end of the book. He only existed for this book, and that's it. That's how I feel about it. The book ended, and poof, he's gone now.

Marina: Yeah, I agree.

Sara: What did you guys think about that lack of backstory, lack of character development with him?

Christie: We only got two small glimpses into his past. One was when he talked about his mom. It was the scene when his mom was vacuuming while he was watching TV. Carroll mused about feeling that he was able to observe things from the outside while not being present in real life. He compared his experience to being on the periphery watching. He then talked about how his mother would go out on a date and she would come back late. He was afraid that she would not come back at all. Then he alluded to the disappearance of his father who did the same thing, except he did not come back.

Sara: On a similar token, did you ever feel legitimately threatened by Caroll or was he just a total naive virginal character? Because I never felt threatened, even when he touched Stevie's nipple or yelled at the other stripper. Even like in these moments when he's yelling at the other stripper for not giving him enough time. That's the final straw that gets him kicked out of Indiscretions. But still I never felt threatened by Carroll.

Christie: I didn't either.

Marina: That's a really great question, the way it's phrased... "threatened"...I do feel that he's part of a misogynistic culture and that...not only does he call women "girls" but idolizes prepubescent looking shaved adult women.

Sara: Can I speak about...shaved for a second? I have a theory about that...because Stevie is the only girl that is shaved at Indiscretions. Well, I seriously think that there are so many religious images in this that I really think she was supposed to be the ideal virgin. And I think that's why she's the only one that shaved. I don't think it was a prepubescent thing.

Christie: Well I would say that I didn't feel threatened by him in as much as he was ever going to do anything that would hurt anyone. I didn't feel threatened by him in that sense. I didn't believe he was going to become physically violent. But as far as him as a person, I agree that he is way off base with a lot of his thinking. I agree that he was misogynistic because of some of the words he was using, the way he treated people, and his thoughts. However, I read Carroll's character as delusional and he was very contradictory in the things he would say. Sometimes he would almost immediately contradict himself. I can't remember the exact situation or the phrasing he used but he was internally judging and critiquing some of the other men. Then he would turn around and behave in the exact same way and think there was nothing wrong with it. The contradictions in thought and actions happened frequently. It left me wondering about his mental state. Was he mentally ill in addition to the anxiety and some of the other stuff that we saw going on? I feel that he was not completely healthy.

Sara: I think he was so childlike and naive. I think he's a virgin for sure. There's no way this guy has gotten laid before—

Christie: He even commented at one point saying something to the effect that his interaction with Stevie was the closest he'd ever been to somebody and he had never even touched anyone.

Sara: Yeah and he said something about like 'what do I know about sex?' He doesn't know anything about sex. And I think that a lot of what you're talking about with the delusion and the misogyny, is because he was just too naive to even see himself or see what was going on. As you were mentioning when he'd look at other guys at the strip club and be like 'Oh I'm not like them.' But he was just like them. But he just couldn't see himself. He was so invisible to the world... to the strippers, to his bosses. I think he's even invisible to himself. Cellophane from *Chicago* that everyone looks right through....no one sees him and he can't even see himself or what he's doing.

Marina: Is his last name Trump?

Christie: No it was Mine. His name was Carroll Mine. But the new cocktail waitress did refer to him as Trump once.

Marina: And there's a description here of the way that the strippers are guided to look to get extra table dances. It's on page 144 at the very bottom. The bottom of 144...yes it's Stevie talking..."To you, I'm supposed to look like I'm having the time of my life, but to the other customers I'm supposed to look like I'm waiting for someone more exciting to dance for. They told me this when I auditioned. I don't know what it means, but if you look when a girl dances [...] she'll a lot of times drop her smile when she turns away from the booth". This description is perfect for how a high-end stripper is instructed. Do you remember Melania Trump at the Inauguration? <u>This meme went viral</u>. She's standing in her blue suit, maybe going for the Jackie Look. She smiles and then boom! Talk about dropping a smile and revealing the performative aspect of gender within a power dynamic.

Sara: Yikes.

Marina: If it makes a novel relevant...

Sara: So put Caroll in our society today. Where would he be? Where would he fit in our society now?

Christie: He would be on the fringes for sure. I think it was you, Sara, who said that you see him as naive. I don't necessarily see him that way. He does have some level of naiveté but I don't see that as a primary characteristic. I see a lot more of the mental health issues, the anxiety, and the delusional episodes. Going back to what I was saying earlier about the ending when he lets loose, I felt like he was unleashing a different side of himself. I can almost imagine him doing something extreme, maybe not in a mass murderer sort of way, but where he just jumps off the deep end and his life spirals out of control. If the book continued beyond the ending and we watched this character unfold and watched this new side of him take over the previously suppressed side of him, who would he become? What would he become? Would he become someone who does something extreme? I can just imagine his life unraveling in a catastrophic way.

Marina: You know I thought that O'Brien was going for a Kafka-like voice, focusing on and magnifying a single incident. It might have been an attempt, albeit unsuccessful, to establish a narrative of transition. As I mentioned, Carroll, who does mind-numbing work, thinks he's being seen as an insect, and then, toward the end, by the Dumpster, I thought of Sartre's *Nausea*. Maybe we can talk about this later..But he doesn't really develop these wonderful gems. They drop off. Again, respect the reader, don't cut the line, keep going. So I feel like there is a lack of discipline.

Sara: I wanted to touch on the loneliness a little from my perspective. I wrote an essay about this book for Rob and what my essay focuses on is addiction and about the loneliness thing, I think Carroll almost wouldn't know what to do if he wasn't lonely. I feel like he's lonely and that's who he is and he doesn't know how to be anything else. But that also fits in with my theory that he's also an addict that does not want rehab. Given the choice of getting clean, he wouldn't. He would choose to continue being an addict going to *Indiscretions* if he could with the loneliness. I just don't I don't think he could be anything but lonely. He's addicted to loneliness.

Marina: I think you are focusing on the character, and I'm focusing on the writing.

Sara: The writing is tough. We could go on and on about the head hopping. You're not generally supposed to jump character perspectives on the same page.

Marina: No but that's cool, it just has to be deliberate. Do you guys know who the storyteller, who the narrator is?

Sara: The narrator changes. Arguably the narrator is John.

Marina: Yeah, but it's in the third person.

Sara: I know, I know.

Marina: So it's limited, intimate, but all of the sudden it shifts to… I forgot if it's just Stevie but maybe some other women in the bar?

Sara: He does.

Marina: But he so doesn't get them. We never get an authentic perspective from any single woman in this novel. They're all girls. None of them is a woman.

Sara: It's funny because when Rob gave me this book to read he wanted me to look out for misogyny. That was the first thing he said he's like "can you tell me how sexist this is?" He wanted me to get my opinion on it.

Marina: You notice it. It's prevalent.

Sara: Christie, what did you think about the sexism in this book?

Christie: I didn't focus on it just because I felt that the sexism was a given. Most guys who frequent strip clubs on a regular basis generally aren't men who respect women. I see strip clubs as a place that promotes the objectification of women.

Marina: Is it possible to want to go to a strip club and yet respect women?

Christie: That's a tough question. First of all, I'm not a man and I don't know a man's intentions and motivations for going to a strip club. I can imagine that they vary quite a bit. I suppose you could still respect women if you were a buddy going along with a group to a strip club just because that's what everyone else is doing and you were not participating. But I find it very problematic just how objectified the women are at a strip club. Going back to Carroll and what he thinks of the women, what he sees in Stevie, and how he critiques every single woman. For example, he talks about the one dancer that he said looks like a housewife. The reason he labels her that way is because her breasts are so small. He sits there and dissects them all, objectifies them all, breaks them down by their body parts, and determines how valuable their anatomy is or isn't.

Sara: But what I was shocked by was that even though he was doing exactly what you're saying it never felt sexual.

Marina: He's almost mimicking the other guys.

Christie: During the table dance Carroll even talked about the fact that he didn't have the ability to have an erection, and maybe he might have one later. I think that was the only reference to him being or even hoping to be sexually stimulated. So you bring up an interesting point. Going back to your previous question, what was his motivation for going to Indiscretions? Carroll even at one point towards the beginning said he'd been going for two years. Every single day. So what was his motivation? Carroll also talked about the routine of it and how he did not want to miss any of the goings-on of the strip club. So in some respect, he almost seemed like a monitor trying to keep tabs on who was there and what was going on.

Sara: That's what I took the addiction from, because the way he talked about *Indiscretions* was like an addict talks about getting their fix. I have to be there every night. He got panicked if he thought about not being there. My brother is an addict, so I am living with this right now, and the things that Carroll would say about like, 'I have to be there at this time...on my parking spot..'if his routine was disrupted at all it was panic mode and that's such an addict's behavior.

Sara: I saw it as an addictive behavior for sure especially knowing what I know about John O'Brien. Once I learned about how he was an alcoholic, and how he was very focused on his drinking schedule, I feel like he mimics that with Carroll but with the strip club which is why when he goes cold turkey and he throws up in an alley it just felt so much like this relapse where he was like giving up his drug.

Marina: Exactly, that's why I thought he was an alcoholic all along.

And it was a relapse and that euphoric ending doesn't really happen..

Sara: I think it's a sad ending, not euphoric.

Marina: Euphoria is sad.

Sara: Ohhh, I like this!

Marina: You know you feel euphoric warmth right before you freeze to death?

Sara: Oh, interesting, I hope I don't ever find that out personally....I thought it was a tragic ending because, in the end, he gets to talk to Stevie and she becomes a real woman with a real name and then it's over. Now he doesn't want to see her or won't see her again because she's become something real.

Marina: And I don't think that really happens. I think it's a glimpse into his own maturity that he has for a moment, but he relapses into drinking.

Sara: Damn! This could go on way too long If we're not careful.

Christie: Can I throw out a question? I have something that I am kind of curious about. I was doing some additional reading about John O'Brien and he had actually used the name Carroll Mine as a pseudonym. Did you know that?

Sara: It's also the name of one of his childhood friends.

Christie: That part I did not know. So I was curious as to why he used the name Carroll Mine. I didn't see this as him trying to write about himself but it was interesting that he chose to use that name rather than come up with a new or original name. I'm curious if you had any thoughts about why he chose the name Carroll Mine for the main character.

Sara: Well according to Erin, his sister, when he was younger, he went by "Johnny" and he worked in a law firm as a clerk-in Cleveland. And so this is Erin's favorite book of his because she said this is the only book that is "Johnny" before the addiction, before the darkness, before he started the downward spiral to suicide. So I think maybe part of choosing that name was, either consciously or subconsciously, John trying to regain that young, innocent part of himself that was gone.

Christie: That would play into some of the conversations you were having around him being a naive character.

Sara: When John was in the law firm he was like 17 or 18 because he left Cleveland when he was 18 to go to Los Angeles. So maybe he just was redrawing this part of his past that he had lost and already knew he was never getting back. So maybe that's why he chose that name? But I know Carol also was a childhood friend of the family. The O'Brien family. But that's kind of my take on it. I've been very lucky because I've gotten to spend a lot of time with Erin over the past few months since I'm writing about John, so it's been nice getting that kind of interior look at him as a person through his sister's eyes. One of my best friends is a stripper. And so obviously I interviewed her also for this. She sees stripping as empowering. She feels that women are empowered by stripping; they become divine figures that loom above the populace literally because they're onstage but also because they have so much sexual power over their audience. So I thought that was interesting. That's how my girlfriend sees her job.

Sera: She really thinks like she is the one with the power.

Christie: You know it's interesting hearing you say that because it goes back to some of the comments that we've heard Stevie make during the table dances. She talks about how at a certain point during a table dance she wins over the customer to the point that she could zigzag his head every which way with her nipples. Stevie also comments to herself and wonders why the men at the strip club do this to themselves. Why do they spend so much money on the strippers? She recognizes that Carroll probably doesn't make a lot of money even before she gets to know him and what he does for a living. She wonders why the men blow their lunch money at the club. So that does speak to the kind of power that the strippers have over the men. They take their money and hypnotize them.

Marina: I think it's a question of who owns the means of production. If the strippers had a co-op strip club and made their own rules and provisions for healthcare and retirement I would feel that it can be empowering, but if they're working for someone like O'Brien calls a "Fat Fuck", then it's not—no matter what story they want to tell themselves.

Sera: Start it up! You're new career! Perfect! You're gonna be a powerful madam of a Cleveland strip club. I love it.

Marina: I would want everyone to have equal ownership.

Sara: That's a good idea. I'll pitch that to my girlfriend.

Sara: So next question. Hypothetical question. We've touched on this. Add your own final chapter. I'd like to hear everyone's take?

Marina: Last page. Who is he talking to? Oh, those two men, the douchebags. So the novel bookends. It starts in darkness and it ends in darkness..."but not really". At one point, O'Brien sort of breaks the fourth wall and asks the reader if they've seen enough. And then, "think about what you are, what there is to see." That's one of my favorite quotes in this novel. Another one is "there are bad days and good days, and they're all part of the same day". So true. Back to this one, "think about what you are, what there is to see." I can just meditate on that for a very long time, and generate a lot of ideas...

"Not so hard anymore, you could walk away, like an intrepid buck." If he was a little bit more disciplined he would have elaborated just slightly on that, or he would have dropped that in earlier and returned to it, and it wouldn't have been contrived had he done it. You could do it in a subtle way. Instead, all the sudden, there's this great analogy—"an intrepid buck, only smarter, on the highway, caught in a headlight". And again that refrain, "seen enough". This is such a beautiful paragraph. Lovely ironic content. I love it. And then Carroll asks, "seen enough? Is that the best you can do? I mean question-wise." That seems like such a meta-narrative twist, right?

I think if I were to extend that—I sort of like it the way it is—but if I were to extend it, I would pick up where Carroll is, squatting then sitting on a plastic dairy crate, and none of that nice stuff between Jennifer a.k.a. Stevie actually happens, and I would end it in the dark. Like a relapse.

Sara: What about you Christie?

Christie: I'm not sure that I'm totally in agreement that the thing with Stevie/Jennifer ever really happened. But at the same time, I don't think they're going to go off into the sunset together. At the bottom of page 200 when Stevie/Jennifer offers to meet Carroll at the coffee shop, he's hesitant.

"After work?" he says, hesitantly.

She laughs, too cute. "What's the matter?" she wants to know, but it's friendly, kidding- like. Whatever he wants, it's all a joke. This guy really is okay, and she's really got to get to work. "Don't you want me?"

Her words float over the gravel like feathers after a pillow fight. *Don't you want me?*

x

Does he?

It is almost like the attraction is all in the chase. Or going back to Carroll's struggle with anxiety and social interactions, I think his interest in Stevie is wonderful when it was just fantasy. However the minute it becomes reality it is overwhelming and he runs. Whether or not she shows up the coffee shop, I don't think he would. I don't think he would have the balls to go through with it. I also don't know that he really does even want her anymore now that the fantasy of it all is gone.

Sara: Erin O'Brien says that this book is about finding and losing your religion. That's what she thinks it's about. And I tend to agree with her on that because he finds his religion in Stevie the angel on stage. He gets lost in a church parking lot for Christ Sake. And then as soon as he as he meets Jennifer he realizes that God is a lie and then that's the end. So I do see where Erin is coming from as far as losing your religion...

Marina: His false idols.

Sara: When you finally meet God you realize he can't save you.

Marina: He puts her on a pedestal, he wants too much. Maybe it was Nietzsche who said "we are most unfair to God; we do not allow Him to sin."

Sara: I will say, if I was going to write a last scene (because Carol only exists within the pages of this novel), the final scene for me would be Stevie's showing up to an empty cafe. He just never shows because he doesn't exist anymore....he's gone. It's a little metaphorical and weird and trippy but I think she goes to the coffee shop and he doesn't...

Interestingly enough John O'Brien was an atheist and he was going through DTs. He always used to see demons coming through the walls. And then one time when he had the DTs, demons were coming through the walls and an angel showed up and said we've lost you but we're going to find you again. Those were the things he saw in DTs, angels and demons...

Marina: How do we know this?

Sara: It's been written about in articles...so yes I was thought that was interesting that his DTs contained religious imagery when he was an atheist. And then he writes this book that's full of religious imagery.

Christie: Even that comment about what the angels said sounds threatening to me rather than reassuring. "You're lost and we're going to find you." That sounds like "I am going to hunt you down."

Marina: And some of the most threatening people to me are overzealous...

Christie: I agree.

Marina: That's the thing. If it is about finding and losing religion, he has an immature idea of people and morality. And he feels that you're either going to be this clean-shaven angel on a pedestal or you're like this demon, and that's immature.

Sara: Caroll is immature.

Marina: We created the idea of God, and in this creation we need to give it some slack.

Sara: I did want to touch on something that really was very jarring and yet I loved it. The one part when it goes into first person POV the first time he sees Stevie. Remember that part? It's pretty much the most beautiful writing in the whole book. It's the most romantic writing in the whole book at least.

It's very early and I just felt very jarred but the writing was so good. It was so interesting that he changed to the first person which changed the tone. It lasts about four pages. It's this beautiful, poetic prose. Thoughts?

Marina: It goes back to his father. The same imagery of an angel goes back to his father in the hot tub scene where he's like, here's a lady in the hot tub that's akin to the angel he sees in Stevie

Sara: I didn't care. I wasn't offended by it. I was just like this is beautiful. So I don't care. It's definitely making a statement that this is important. Pay attention, I'm switching POV.

Christie: I have to say that I didn't even notice. I was reading with a focus on something else. I didn't notice the change in point of view. I was actually reading it and seeing the hypocrisy within what he was saying. I didn't see this as beautiful and poetic.

Marina: I found it cannibalistic and desperate, "her perspiration is sweet water, and I would lick it". I was embarrassed for him. I'm hoping he'd take a drink.

Sara: Maybe because I write erotica for my job I'm like Yeah! Lick that sweat!

Marina: I like erotica when it's authentic. His drinking is authentic. Was O'Brien married, or did he have a girlfriend in real life?

Sara: He was married to a wonderful woman who would walk over fire for him. They got divorced.

Christie: After 13 years, right? It was a long time.

Sara: Yeah. They got divorced. They got divorced and Erin said he'd be dead within six months and he was dead within a year. He was happily married for a long time. I did embarrassingly have to ask his sister is her brother frequented strip clubs. It was a fair question, and she said she didn't know but, as someone who does frequent strip clubs myself, I know he must have done research, quote-unquote, because it's too real for him to just have made this up. So I know he did research but I don't think it was like an issue, he wasn't addicted to strip clubs or anything but he was he was very observant based on the writing of this.

Christie: I wanted to bring up something that I thought was interesting. Going back to just before he changes his point of view on page 28. No one else looks to be very interested, and Carroll wonders if this could mean Stevie has already danced tonight, danced for them when he wasn't around. The curtain maintains its high pressure, then it is parted by a hand, an arm, a leg. Like the girl is on stage. The room falls briefly to attention—a blond head will do this. But then some of the men drift back into their conversations, content with glancing at the stage every few seconds as a way to introduce punctuation into whatever it is they're saying. Not them, Carroll is smitten.

So here it talks about how nobody else was really paying attention, but he is. This makes me wonder about how special Stevie really is? What does Carroll see in her? Remember the new red-headed dancer towards the end of the novel? We never learned her name because Carroll is beginning to unravel but the rest of the club was completely enthralled with her. Carroll talked about how if he didn't have Stevie he probably would have been under her spell. It just made me wonder how arbitrary his infatuation with Stevie was. I don't know that it was really Stevie that was so special. It could have been any woman.

Sara: So what I have conflict with is why Stevie and I still don't have an answer. If you look at my copy of *Stripper Lessons*, there are so many questions about why Stevie?

Christie: I feel like if Stevie hadn't shown up this night then it would have been the redhead that Carroll became infatuated with. The way that he talks about the redhead and describes her, it sounds like he could have gone there with her. So I feel like it wasn't necessarily about Stevie. The infatuation was more likely caused by something internal within himself. Maybe he was just to the point where he was ready to find this attachment or obsession.

Sara: Before we move on, I did want to say one thing about the arrival of Stevie and maybe it wasn't her, but something inside of him. I liked the parallel with the Bombgate file so all of that was going on at the same time.

Maybe it was something with that where he's seeking, he's seeking, he's seeking this stupid empty file at work. He's seeking some kind of connection at the club and it all felt empty and a very obvious parallel in the end. The file is empty in the end. He has nothing left. So maybe it's something...

Christie: Not to mention the whole search was futile because it didn't seem like it was even needed. This is another instance where you ask yourself "What was the point?" The client thought that the whole Bombgate situation was dead, and at the meeting, it didn't seem like it was being addressed. Pam had made it seem so urgent and needed, but at the end, she just brushed it off by saying something like "Well let's just be satisfied with this. They didn't need it anyway."

Marina: But that's corporate absurdity right. I'm okay with that.

Sara: And also the futility of seeking.

Marina: Yes! And then on page 62...My God his repetition of Angel. Again and again and again. Are you an angel? I just wanted to slap Carroll like you pathetic fuck, grow up.

Sara: Well it is. What else do we want to talk about?

Marina: So you know I would love to talk more about the writing, the word choice...like he uses the word *propitious*. Yeah, *propitious* a whole bunch of times.

Sara: These things an editor would have caught. The problem with editing a dead guy's work is that you don't change it. And I think that's something that they had to deal with and Erin has talked about with the editing of this book because those are things an editor would have caught and changed because I know my editor yells at me if I use the word *headed, headed in that direction*. She hates it and she'll underline those things. So she catches those things but I think as an editor if you're editing someone's book posthumously it's a terrifying thing about messing it up. And so I think those are things that would have been cleaned up in an editorial process if the author had input and was not deceased.

Marina: Was *Leaving Las Vegas* edited?

Sara: Yeah that came out when he was alive

Marina: He was open to working with an editor?

Sara: I would think so because it was through a traditional publishing house. So yeah that one was before he passed away. This is the light happy book comparatively. Based on this book would you read other books by John O'Brien?

Christie: Yes I would, I'm curious now.

Marina: Me too.

Christie: I probably would start with *Leaving Las Vegas* just because it was the only one that he completed and fully brought to fruition.

Marina: I heard *Assault On Tony* was strong.

Sera: I'm good. Anything else we'd like to discuss?

Marina: I liked the chapter titles.

Christie: I did too.

Marina: I would link Carroll with the loner who frequents brasseries in Jean-Paul Sartre's novel, *Nausea,* except *Stripper Lessons* kind of misses an existential epiphany or deliverance like at the end of *Nausea* with the Chestnut tree and the whole of existence within its gnarly texture. And that's why my answer to that really great question you asked, how would you finish it, is to take him back to the "crepitant gravel", to the vomit, to the kneeling, to the whole texture of it all. The relapse. I would take it back to that. I'm not an addict, and I don't think, no matter how empathetic you are, if you're not an addict you don't know what it's like. But I do know that as a writer, you've got to respect the reader.

Sara: *Publishers Weekly* really hated this book because they said nothing happened.

Marina: Well, I don't see that.

Sara: They basically just said it's a bunch of words and nothing happens.

Christie: I don't agree that nothing happened. I think something happened for Carroll. I'm thinking back to your idea that he was only completely contained within this novel. I don't know that I would have read it that way, that he doesn't exist outside of the book cover. Even if that is the case, something definitely happened within him. He didn't really affect the world or even affect Stevie for that matter. It barely affected anybody else that he was working with at the law firm, but it certainly affected him.

Sara: I don't agree with *Publishers Weekly,* that was just their take on it.

I just had a thought. I know we keep talking more and more because it's fun to talk about this. Stevie doesn't have to work. She has a man who has paid for her apartment. Who is paying for everything she does? She has sex occasionally and that's their relationship. Why do you think she works?

Christie: I wondered that too. Stevie was talking about wanting to save money. Maybe this is too obvious, but I wondered if she wanted to leave her boyfriend. The relationship was very adversarial. As far as I could see there didn't seem to be any enjoyment in it from either side. I even wondered why was the man supporting her and continuing the relationship because he didn't seem to be enjoying the relationship either. Neither side seemed to be getting much from it but they continued on anyway. Maybe Stevie is just ready to move on.

Sara: What do you think about Stevie's reasons for working?

Marina: I don't know her backstory. Again my view of how the novel is sexist isn't really as much about objectifying female characters as it is about not not giving them a voice. I mean, I find *To Kill A Mockingbird* racist even though it's considered a very anti-racist novel. It doesn't allow a fully human perspective, a three-dimensional voice of a single character of color. Likewise, I don't see a single female in *Stripper Lessons* who's fully human. So, why did Stevie do what she did? Because I think the author wasn't interested in this.

Sara: Good point. I think that's all I have.

Christie: I just want to say one thing before we completely close. I want to continue what we were saying about Stevie and developing any one of these women into a character. We don't know very much about Stevie, just like we don't have any backstory on Carroll. However there's that one scene towards the end when her boyfriend visits her, and we get her perspective after they had sex. She's on the balcony and the semen is leaking from her and she alludes to having a hysterectomy. She talks about how much the surgery hurt initially, and now she's just numb. I read a lot into that. I was thinking about how she just feels numb. I don't think she meant only physically numb. I think she felt emotionally and spiritually numb as well. I wondered why O'Brien added this when he hasn't given us any real insights into her at all. It was a little glimmer into her as a character, and then the book just shifted and moved on.

Marina: Yeah, isn't that easier? To just numb her.

Christie: Absolutely.

Sara: I'm sorry. I would like to speak but I'm too busy thinking about what you just said. I really liked that scene. I kind of forgot about it and so right now I really like that part. Honestly just the imagery, the sensory details felt very real and sad.

Marina: I mean, we have more information about her cuticle than about her life.

Sara: That's true. I love those details, those little details are really cool.

Marina: Again, it's the writer's choice. That's something he likes to focus on.

Sara: But also maybe maybe one of his choices was keeping an emotional distance from the female characters because that's what Carroll was doing.

Marina: "Here comes Tasha for her take". What kind of sentence is that? I'm looking at the writing.

Sarah: I don't know, overall I'll give it a thumbs up. I enjoyed the experience of reading this book. I enjoyed writing about this book.

A Review of Stripper Lessons

Carolyn Jack

Apparently, John O'Brien lived a short, anguished life. Most readers of record have viewed the novels he left behind as autobiographies of sorts, or at least skeleton keys to the forever locked-away impulses and reasons that made him a desperate alcoholic, a writer and a suicide at the age of 33.

That's a tempting perspective, first because O'Brien created some characters with obvious parallels to himself, as so many writers do, but second because regarding any work as a roman à clef makes it easier to swallow and digest. Explicating art by comparing it to the artist's life can be useful: The echoes of real-life events and experiences, of demonstrated preoccupations and relationships give savor and tang to the invented ones, wrap them in a ready-made context that helps the audience or reader consume easily and with satisfaction.

Reading novels as autobiography is interesting. But it's also superficial, yielding only an incidental part of the story. You get the whole enchilada only if you look at that enchilada as a thing unto itself – a work, a world, an idea that succeeds or fails on its own structure and content, with no bottled sauce to help it go down.

So what is the whole enchilada of Stripper Lessons?

Almost 21 years ago, I reviewed the book for The Plain Dealer. It had been released three years after O'Brien's death – an unfinished work that Erin O'Brien, the author's sister, had arranged to have published. I had not read any other O'Brien works at that time, nor seen the film version of Leaving Las Vegas, and still have not. Back then, I had never met either of the O'Briens and knew only the most basic facts about John's life. Still haven't – except for a business e-mail I sent to Erin O'Brien in August 2018 – and don't. I consumed

Stripper Lessons in 1997, and again in June 2018, as if it were a unique dish.

And, uniquely, it works. Not because it offers any clues as to why O'Brien drank and killed himself. Not because it resembles, or elaborates upon, his prior novels – I wouldn't know. And not because it's pleasing on a technical level, for there is no polished craftsmanship or sophisticated technique here.

The whole enchilada of Stripper Lessons is emotional truth: odd, stunted emotion, yes, barely detectable at times and maybe even a little pathological, but palpably, movingly true. It makes the book the equivalent of street food, something thrown together a little crudely, something served on a stick or in a paper boat. Something tasty and real. I bet Anthony Bourdain would have loved Stripper Lessons.

Had he lived, O'Brien might have learned more of the niceties of fiction writing. He tells the story of Stripper Lessons in awkward, herky-jerky, third-person interior monologue; the narrator shares head space with main character Carroll Mine, a youngish file clerk who wants to connect with other people, but suffers from such extreme self-consciousness, self-criticism and constant, paralyzing embarrassment that he just can't. This narrator sounds as if he's speaking in Carroll's voice, a strange mix of strained and clumsy syntax, mangled ordinary-guy expressions and random spelling-bee words that suggest higher intelligence of a sporadic kind, as if a radio signal from a highly advanced alien civilization is randomly crossing signals with some tired classic-rock station in Enid, Okla. Occasionally, and for no apparent reason, this same narrator turns up briefly in the heads of other characters whose thoughts Carroll has no way of knowing.

These are the mistakes of an amateur, yet their effect is weirdly masterful: Carroll Mine feels like a real person, an emotionally disadvantaged, tamely obsessive, timid, good-hearted, tedious, really-real person that you'd like to help if you only had the patience. What

171

saves Carroll and the book, what makes it good street food and not rubbish, is that the important characters change themselves. Not miraculously. Only a little. Yet that slight change feels hard-earned and believable, prosaic and yet poignant – genuine through and through.

John O'Brien nails this. (In reply to my 2018 e-mail, Erin O'Brien, who is also a writer, assured me that she had made no content changes to the manuscript of Stripper Lessons.) His story understands how real people react and behave. His characters' simple willingness to be humane in the end, to do each other the tiny favor of saying yes rather than no, of not being luridly fearful, mean, violent and destructive despite their weary and unrewarding lives, carries you through Carroll's dreary existence to something better. As he moves endlessly and anonymously between his dull, dead-end job at a law firm and his habitual, fixated lurking at the shadowy edges of a strip club, goals emerge: to find a lost file at work and to speak to Stevie, a stripper he likes. Pathetically and almost imperceptibly, Carroll finds something like purpose, something like pride in his effort. A hint of agency and determination slowly color his nearly invisibility with form, wavery but identifiable. He learns to try.

He reaches out just as Stevie, disappointed in her life, learns to let someone in. There is no crashing climax, no ardor. They agree to meet for coffee, the simplest, most everyday human connection on the planet. It is important only to them and moving only to the reader. Carroll and Stevie are just getting on with their lives, only now with something like a friend.

And that's the enchilada in toto. Nothing fancy. Nothing big. You don't need to hear a single fact about John O'Brien's life to get his point. Lessons, indeed.

Desolation Angels
David Megenhardt

Let's take a moment to meditate on strippers and prostitutes. I fear I've lost half of you with that first sentence, at least the women readers of this book, because can we seriously consider the tawdry world strip clubs and the shadows and motels where whores ply their trade without out motives being questioned? You might offer, with a knowing wink, that you can understand why a straight man might want to while away his time in a literary essay thinking about young(ish) naked women whose sole purpose is to titillate and satiate. But our job, together you and I, are to be taken seriously in our collective pursuit, so let's agree that we are not trying to get our rocks. Our aim is not so much to dwell on the minutiae of the professions, however pleasurable that might be, but to explore how O'Brien uses these filthy angels (in O'Brien's low worlds I don't believe there can be any other kind) as central figures in both *Stripper Lessons* and *Leaving Las Vegas*.

For those of you who have taken the plunge with me let's admit we are entering dangerous territory, a roiling river of sin crusted over with the thinnest veneer of ice (or cum depending on the depravity of your metaphors) on which we tread. I'm not writing of the sin of a naked woman on a stage dancing to a priapic congregation willingly tithing until their wallets, and possibly bank accounts, are as empty as their social lives. No the sin of which I speak is using a strip club as a crutch in a narrative. I confess I can't really think of a book with a strip club scene in it, but that may be more of a product of my idiosyncratic reading lists than an exhaustive search leading to no results. I haven't read much gritty detective fiction, so scores of scenes could be out there without my knowledge. This is where, believe it or not, an online comment section would be functional as the hive mind would gleefully correct me by citing their favorite strip club scenes from their bookshelves. Exactly how satisfying is to write a strip club scene though? Does it have the same effect as it does in a movie, injecting a sudden charge of titillation or at best eroticism into a story even if it has nothing to do with the plot? Until a conversation can take place with the society of book snobs who happen to know the very best strip club scenes in the literary canon. Of course, we could include Salomé in our discussion, at least the Richard Strauss and Oscar Wilde version of her: the iteration of Salomé who dances with seven veils, then six, five…until her glorious body is revealed. Staged properly, the dance turns into a striptease of horrific proportions, climaxing with Salomé kissing the severed head of John the Baptist. Wilde and Strauss charge the tale with erotic portent, absent from the Gospel account (Mark 6: 21-22), which reads:

> Finally, the opportune time came. On his birthday Herod gave a banquet for his high officials and military commanders and the leading men of Galilee. When the daughter of[b] Herodias came in and danced, she pleased Herod and his dinner guests.

Indeed, that description will never concentrate blood flow, but Wilde imagined other possibilities as he staged the tale, brought the version of Salomé to life as painted by Gaston Bussiere, Henri Regnault, Jean Sala, Gustave Moreau, Pierre Bonnard, Jean Benner, Leon Herbo, Francesc Masriera and many more. Visual artists are drawn to the story for obvious reasons and in our time movies have replaced painting as the visual form appropriate to both Salomé and the striptease. One only has to watch Rita Hayworth take a turn as Salomé to understand the possibilities although one grieves that in her performance the seventh veil uncovers an eighth veil in the form of a negligee that keeps her form sheathed in the standards of her time. Unlucky us that Rita Hayworth was born a generation or two too early.

Given the visual nature of the performance let's focus awhile on the traps of film that await a screenwriter or director who does not have the grounding of a Bible story to interpret or the climax of all prophets in the body and severed head of the Baptist on which to rely. What erection could ever compete with the snuffing out of the man who has seen the coming of Christ? Naked or barely clothed women dancing are a pleasing sight, without a doubt in most everyone's mind, so why not figure out ways of inserting such a pleasing sight whenever one can without the need of a proceeding scene to get the woman naked; no date, no prelude, no wooing, just set the characters in front of a stage with a pole and a director has a vehicle for nudity at their disposal; some are not so transparent in their aims. Take, for example, Antonioni's *La Notte* during which married couple Jeanne Moreau and Marcello Mastroianni visit a strip club, and as they stare at the gyrating dancer, their faces reflect both their failed marriage and animal lust. They look miserable but actively looking for a way out. Unfortunately, not all directors are as smart as Antonioni and see not the stripper as a symbol, but as an excuse to insert tits and ass in their lame movie. Put a well-formed pair of breasts behind action that could just as easily taken place in a coffee shop or public park the director stands a chance of keeping the audience awake. Unlike *La Notte*, such scenes serve no other purpose. Even whole movies have been scripted this purpose, such as *Showgirls*. A delusional colleague of mine has argued for a reassessment of the movie, which has garnered something akin to cult status since its stunning failure upon release, marred by terrible dialogue and an equally bad plot. The movie misses the point of exalting the female form and focuses on the dumb rise and fall of slimy idiots. The movie is ashamed of its intent, so it turns toward power and greed, commoditizing the body without honesty. If we could come to grips with our desire and need to exalt the female form, strip clubs would resemble houses of worship, solemn, serious, shrouded in ceremony and mystery with angelic guides initiating the acolytes into the cult. In a way, these clubs attempt such a transformation, except they are designed by architects sporting gold chains in a thicket of chest hair and an ever-expanding paunch under a satin shirt. They are houses that pimps build when they have a little business moxie. The women are captives in male fantasy, not empowered by the lure of their flesh. The "high class" places are advertised as gaudy dens of excess where successful men of money order females like they would a shot of top-shelf liquor, a brothel without the sex, where the women are young, nubile, and cast themselves as characters to enhance the thrill (the Brit or vaguely European immigrant on an American tour, fresh college girls working their way from school, the femme fatale, the neighborhood girl who likes nothing more than fucking, etc.). The worst of these places are straight-up brothels, taverns gone to seed, throwing naked women at the broke clientele as a last resort before bankruptcy. The patrons bet the over/under on caesarian scars and track marks. There is no acting here, no characters, just transactions. The dance is an advertisement for a blowjob in the parking lot or a fuck in a nearby motel if the dude had been recently paid. Cops make easy arrests when they are bored and take easy payoffs. The pimp owners exploit our most ancient needs. These outcasts own these businesses we've repressed ourselves under a hundred layers of horseshit, and we punish those willing to become archeologists of base desire. Generally, city planners, if they must, zone these clubs by freeways at the outer edges of commercial districts, wastelands between self-storage units, dollar stores and heavy equipment rental warehouses places that seem appropriate to dumping corpses or used tires. Occasionally, one can find one in a prime downtown location in cities that are natural picks for conventions where officials traded zoning for a bag of cash. They are treated as a resident virus that can never entirely be killed, but will never be allowed to consume the entire body.

Stripper Lessons was written before the onset of internet porn, and one wonders if strip clubs will go the way of department stores and video rental chains. The lure of the female form will never diminish as long as there are men, but the need for flesh and blood lap dances certainly will. Sure you can talk to an actual woman for the prices of her drinks as she tries to tame her hardcore hillbilly accent, but can she change her race, hair color, cup size, proportions as she performs the entire milieu of sex acts with a few mouse clicks? The poor stripper has no chance of competing for the attention and money of a generation born and bred on the screen. Even she may not know they're there as she snaps a hundred selfies of herself on the pole as her audience watches porn at the end of the stage, afraid to look at real labia. In the near future, one can imagine an old-timely entertainment complex of bowling alleys, movie theaters, bookstores and strip clubs, stubbornly alive for reasons of nostalgia and kitsch, holding only remnants of their past power to amuse and entertain. The book itself will be an anthropologists treasure to determine how we used to live.

If you're determined to live in a world of decency and puritanism you'll reject these clubs without much deep thought and you'll consign the patrons of such places as perverts and losers, schmucks in sexless marriages, adolescent boys unable to see an entire woman beyond her enticing parts or men who would rather stare at a naked woman than watch another goddamn football game. Maybe that is who they are. Whatever their individual stories the collective atmosphere they create is palpably depressing. Imagine going to church, and the pews are filled with glowering, silent men. On the altar, an angel slits back and forth and slowly peels off her holy raiment. After two overly long hymnals during which the organist leans on the bass, she stands naked before them. She gyrates, squats, lies on her back, legs spread, given unobstructed views for any eyeball brave enough to look. It is not a climax, but an extended tease choreographed to another thudding hymn. For a small donation of a dollar, the congregate can get a close-up view, necessary memories for jacking off in his attic or basement when he gets home. But then the church metaphor collapses under its weight because the minister of a church promises a clear road to salvation, or, at the very least, a manual for clean living, the strip club offers nothing of the sort. All those lovely body parts do not clear your mind, but they do make you a slave to a raging boner and your deep, animal lust. The patron will leave more agitated and confused than when he came in, even if he managed to come in his pants during an especially good lap dance. He has not been given the Word, no guide, no signpost even, but he has seen a glimpse, tasted the first taste, of the author of his destruction, should he care to follow her. She is not a real person. Whatever personality he gave her is from his imagination, a product of fantasy and the cues to tropes she has supplied. Neither is she an angel, and he will realize once his wallet is empty and he has neither the satisfaction of a post-coital embrace nor a hard promise of a future date. Sure he can see her again, after his bank account has been recharged and if she's not busy with another customer. The odds are against him finding anything of worth at the feet of a stripper, but try he must.

Into this maelstrom, O'Brien dives with *Stripper Lessons*, published posthumously in 1997 by Grove Press. O'Brien himself has cast long odds against finding meaning and being taken seriously by centering his action inside a strip club. The literary snobs among have no tradition in which to place a book like this. As previously discussed, writers have avoided strippers like the clap. His peers and forbearers thought nothing could be gained by analyzing such places, so let's consider if O'Brien too should have stayed away also. The novel follows Carroll as he falls into obsession over a dancer named Stevie. When we first meet him, it is clear he is already a regular at a club called Indiscretions. He is man closed upon himself like a clam, so firmly shut he has to work himself up to speak to one of the other patrons, a plan he came into the club armed with. As he watches a naked dancer in front of him, he says, "She has pretty blonde hair," as an opener. The man snorts back, "Not all that blonde, buddy," and the interaction is over. We can guess that Carroll does not fit in the society of men; he has no jocular banter at his disposal. His shyness has crippled him, driven him to the club, but he can go no further just watching. He finds it unfathomable that some men actually purchase a topless table dance as he has been unable to even ask a dancer how much a dance costs let alone close the deal. Not surprisingly he lives alone in a small apartment where even a visit from the maintenance man causes consternation. His aloneness is complete, if hard to relate to. When at the end of the first chapter he leaves the club and ventures back to his apartment, he stands in his underwear trying to emulate a move one of the dancers had made earlier in the night. His interest in naked women is suddenly thrown into question. Is he a heterosexual looking for some fresh material to fuel masturbation or does he see these dancers as guides away from his loneliness, so openly naked in front of strangers, so willing to not be shy, so powerful and athletic and desired: all that he is not. What does it matter if the lesson comes from the other gender in the most unlikely place?

His job as a file clerk at a law office offers him no satisfaction. A file has gone missing, SoLo/Bombgate. Carroll thinks he knows the lawyer who has the file, but he will not admit he has it in his office or that he has misplaced it. The missing file tortures Carroll throughout the book, and we come to understand that his life in all facets is measured out in careful teaspoons. He is J. Alfred Prufrock ordering every aspect of his life, daring not, buying apple cider (not hard) at Indiscretions, calculating the time it takes to sip the drink to make the visit fit within his highly structured budget. The SoLo/Bombgate is out of place and as file clerk suspicion for its disappearance falls on him, but his organization is so exact he knows that he cannot be responsible for its removal. Yet, he is clearly not ready to be consumed by his ordered aloneness. He is driven to the garish and tacky world of Indiscretions, searching for a connection, a release from his misery.

Then he sees Stevie as she performs her first three dance striptease. Carroll appreciates that she is nearly nude during her first dance, dropping all pretense, crafting a dance of no veils. By the second dance, he is thinking of her with biblical undertones, such as "he who would taunt her betrays a blasphemous voice," and that she is "among enemies and those who seek to defile her—save one." It's not much of a leap to Psalm 23 as we think of Stevie walking through the valley of the shadow of death, fearing no evil, and certainly not fearing a collection of leering wolves, licking their chops. She has walked in Carroll's order of the universe as an angel. She is beyond fantasy, beyond an accelerant for masturbatory conflagration. By the third dance, as she stands naked on stage, her pubic hair shaven to reveal her every fold, and Carroll contrasts himself with her. He thinks, "there she stands, more naked than I have ever been, yet untouchable. Her sweat is her garment, mine simply smells. She glistens; I drip. Her perspiration is sweet water and I would chastely lick it from her feet." He later goes on to think, "She walks among men; I crawl." Carroll sees more in her than an object of desire. She embodies everything he is not: fearless, confident, sexual, beautiful and powerful. He does not want to possess her, or God forbid fuck her. No, he wants to worship her perfection and through his devotion become more like her.

A few days later Carroll has a dream during which he is in a hot tub, and a beautiful woman rises from the water naked. He asks her if she is an angel and she confirms that she is, but her answer is unclear when Carroll asks whether the meek shall inherit the earth. We don't know if there is hope for Carroll beyond having a naked woman in his presence. If she has the gift of prophecy, he does not have the capability of deciphering her words.

O'Brien wisely shifts the narration away from Carroll's overheated imagination and follows Stevie through the mundane aspects of the working life of a stripper: chatting about shifts, how to make the most money, tending to a bleeding cuticle, and being thought of by her peers and managers as just another girl hustling for cash. O'Brien is telling us that she is flesh-and-bone and the narration does not agree that Stevie is an angel walking among us, but that Carroll is so vulnerable in his cocoon and he is walking the line between delusion and reality. At this point in the story, we do not know if his imagination is merely the product of being smitten by her stunning visage or something more sinister.

Although no angel. Stevie is kind and genuine, untouched by the enemies around her. Throughout the novel she teaches Carroll to step out of his self-imposed imprisonment, hence the lesson from a stripper. She pulls him out of himself, triggers his aggression, although it's first fitfully manifested. Through the course of chats with her as he sips his ubiquitous apple cider he's drawn closer and closer, his courage emboldened, until he commits a true indiscretion, touching her breast as he is tipping her a dollar for a stage dance. At once, his carefully orchestrated approach explodes, and she retreats from him, categorizing as just another creep unable to keep his hands off her rarified flesh.

Carroll thinks himself dead; his fantasies ripped apart by their impossibility. Freed from his past life he acts out at work. His supervisor tells him that the missing SoLo/Bombgate file has been found, but he knows it is a ruse, that the file has been recreated incompletely, enough to pass by the client, but not a true solution to his disappearance. Because Carroll had already befouled an angel with his greasy hands, he can do anything. He is unmoored, and he bursts into a SoLo/Bombgate client meeting and speaks the unfortunate truth to no one's satisfaction. He's not so much a whistleblower as a confessor of his sins, except there's no one in the room who cares about his confession. There's no priest to lead him to absolution. He's hustled from the room, his job clearly at an end. He has repeated the same indiscretion at work as he did at the club. He has broken through the artifice of rules in both cases. His aggression has led him to act and speak the truth, but both places are built upon something other than truth, and both reject him for his actions.

One can imagine we are about to enter the darkness of an active shooter, of some unspeakable violence, a bloody denouement of a misunderstood life, but suddenly and quite unexpectedly the narrative tension relents. As Carroll is stalking the parking lot of the club, he spies Stevie in her boyfriend's borrowed Ferrari and makes a beeline for her. Instead of consummation in gore, he apologizes for his transgression and ends up securing a date for coffee. To further kill the illusion he finds out her name is Jennifer, like millions of others of her generation, an angel transformed into another girl who could have sat two rows behind him in third grade. Perhaps the story is the reverse of a traditional love story, of having to overcome nakedness and eroticism of an object of desire to find the person underneath instead of the pursuit, the dates, the slow but inevitable march toward nakedness and consummation.

Nevertheless, it is Stevie/Jennifer that saves Carroll from himself. He may have found her in an unlikely place, an impossible place, but angels and teachers can be found anywhere. Better times will be coming for sad sack Carroll, one imagines, all thanks to a naked angel made mortal just for him. An unexpected ending, perhaps false, after the slow rising frustration of the preceding pages, but not every story has to end with a bleak or bloody catharsis.

But some stories do demand such endings, and some women are not necessarily messengers of hope as companions in doom. Enter Sera of *Leaving Las Vegas,* who, unlike Stevie, can claim to be the progeny of a bookshelf full of prostitutes like herself. From the eponymous novels, Fanny Hill and Moll Flanders to Odette in Proust's *In Search of Lost Time* and Sonia Marmeladova in Dostoevsky's *Crime and Punishment* the literary canon have a sub-canon of marvelously rich prostitute characters. So significant is this category that a thorough discussion of these women requires book-length space, so we'll radically truncate our comparisons between Sera and prostitutes of time past and stick to the original point, that O'Brien is staking claim to land well-traveled by writers before him with Sera while he went off course and forged ahead almost alone with Stevie.

Sera is no tease. Within the first few pages of the book, she has been anally raped by three Heineken-fueled college boys. She is a sex worker abused by the perversions of her johns. How different than Stevie's entrance, perfectly naked, wings aloft, absolutely untouchable. She had been touched, again and again, multiple times a night. She is no fantasy projected onto a screen, but a receptacle of release. These boys in their numbered jerseys think nothing of violating her asshole over her repeated protestations. She is scuttling in deep darkness, no longer human in the eyes of those who want her holes, debased and in danger.

The further insult comes as she is punched in the face and two boys piss on her breasts. She carries the bruises on her face throughout most of the novel, a reminder to all of her damage. Even the cabbie who takes her home from this assault mocks her walk, guessing correctly that she has been anally raped and thinking it an appropriate punchline. Whereas Stevie is protected by the rules of the club and the structure of the tableside chats and dances, Sera is alone, navigating a corrupt and brutal world. Her sacred breasts are befouled, and her position in society could not be lower. She carries a pride that she is still alive and that these violations will not put her down. Her friendship with a 15-year-old runaway lasts only a moment before the girl is consumed by heroin. Her friendship with a neighbor continues until Sera admits she is a prostitute. The neighbor complains to the landlord, and Sera is evicted. Sera endures. She lives moment to moment, from one trick to the next, one drink to a session the casinos' tables. Money is transitory, from john to dealer or bartender.

Later on in the story, we find that she is trapped by a pimp/ boyfriend named Gamal Fathi, Al for short, who is the reason she escaped from Los Angeles to Las Vegas. He has followed her to Vegas and demands control once he finds her. She submits without a fight. It is a hopeless life, but O'Brien doesn't write it that way. Sera bears each fresh humiliation without reaction, as if it is all expected or that she has been violated so many times that shock or rage are inconceivable emotions. Beyond feeling animal fear at the hands of the college boys, she faces each new situation with the heart of an adventurer, except she has no grail to find, no island to discover, no magnetic pole to plant a flag upon.

Stevie's body is under glass, to be observed and desired. She is perfect in form striding on stage, elevated and celebrated by her motley congregation with Carroll as the lead acolyte. Her every curve is magnificent and inspected. She is a pinup, a statue with a perfect ass, an airbrushed centerfold. Sera walks through fire as a receptacle of animal desire. She has no congregation, no ritual to protect and exalt her. She stands naked among a jeering crowd, who hate their own desires as much as they hate her. Although she is battered in the face, she still turns tricks. The wounds to her anus open when a fat man pounds away at her as if his penis is a fist. She is to be crushed and humiliated, abused and to be forgotten once she is used up. The only lesson she could teach, beyond the art of endurance, is to never become a prostitute under any circumstances.

Into her life staggers Ben, whose alcoholic suicide has brought him to Las Vegas for the final act. They meet on the strip, Sera hustling, and Ben drunk. They go back to his motel room to attempt to complete the transaction, but Ben is already more interested in a drink than a blowjob. Sera, hollowed-out, a blank space during her interactions with johns, can barely create conversation. However, she can tell that Ben is different than the men who abuse and debase her. From the beginning, he sees her humanity and is unfazed by her status. He has sunk so low she is the only person that he could possibly talk to, the only person who will understand him, and not judge him. He does not want release, but company as he hurtles toward the end.

The next day he tracks her down on the street and asks her out on an old-fashioned date without the meter running, and their brief relationship begins. Ben needs a companion to usher him to his death, a battered angel to hold his head as he vomits the blackness from within. Unlike Carroll, Ben has no illusions of who Sera is, and he sees a person underneath the hooker's clothes and bruises. Who else could play this part except for a prostitute who has survived in darkness with a rush of rapists, perverts, and sadists? Only she could have the requisite knowledge to understand his desire to die; only she could understand life may not be worth living and one answer is to drink yourself into oblivion. But Ben retains too much of his old charm, his besotted life force has not yet been extinguished. As beaten as she is Sera is not immune to his charms and feelings of love as they spend time together.

They cannot stay together long. Sera, the survivor, must turn away when the business of dying starts to get serious. She can see the shards of Ben that have weathered the alcohol, and she ultimately wants to heal him, but that is not the deal on which the relationship began. For Ben, she is the angel who is to provide palliative care. She has no chance of changing his course, of making him try one more time. Ben casts her away by procuring a prostitute and purposely being caught by Sera in flagrante delicto. It is a humiliation that even a battered prostitute cannot endure. Since the aborted blowjob of the first night, they have been celibate. Ben has cast her as a chaste nurse; fucking will somehow soil her part. One suspects a whiff of Catholicism wafting through this arrangement as Sera must be free of sin to usher him to his death. Even if we don't go down the path of heavy-handed symbolism of the church that Sera must be a chaste angel, a friend, to serve her purpose, that consummation with her may bring Ben back toward a life he has decided to leave. He guesses correctly that sex with a whore will would her enough to make her leave. He wants the perfect nurse but ends up with the perfect girlfriend, who he rejects. It is a small mercy from Ben to break off the relationship when the true dying begins, knowing that Sera's strength and resiliency oppose the final act. No one can understand the blackness of a suicide's thoughts and Sera can play along for a time, but even she rebels in the end. She is no nightshade. For her death is to be avoided, not embraced. Once she makes the slightest demand upon him, that he merely consider living, she must go. Ben may be as unrealistic as Carroll when he first sees Stevie on the stage. He does account for her feelings, for her perspective on the play. He wants her to be objective, unemotional, understanding, beautiful, with an in-depth knowledge of the horrors of the world, but she cannot love, she cannot feel, she cannot help him overcome his despair.

In the end, he calls her and she comes to his hotel room, upgraded from the seedy motel where they began so that he can guide him through his final breath. He is at death's door and apologizes for breaking them apart. Glimmers of the old Ben persist. He has lived deliberately, purposefully toward a death of his own making. And for that she loves him, will always love him. As Stevie turned from fantasy angel to Jennifer, Sera moves toward her humanity away from her status as a beaten and broken angel of the street. Sera's admission of love is both sad and hopeful that someone so abused can find connection speaks to the indefatigable nature of the human spirit, that true connection is even possible in a world of misery is a miracle.

Carroll finds his angel and has hope that he will be able to participate in society more fully, outside of his periscopic thoughts. Ben finds his angel—when any prospect of hope, or even the desire to grasp or regain any semblance of hope, had long since passed.

Afterword
Erin O'Brien

This collection is at once mandatory and harrowing. As thorough and diverse as the voices herein are, John languishes as a shadowy figure behind all his words, which is not the fault of the contributors. For the majority of his readers, John is as two-dimensional as the pages he filled, but he was three-dimensional and then some to me. He was my brother, five years my senior. He took his life on April 10, 1994.

How shall I reveal him? Since the details are all that really matters when you're poised at a keyboard, I'll deliver the man hidden between the lines by way of a few of those.

John had two parlor tricks. For his first, he'd find a thick obsolete telephone book, which was abundant in nearly every household during his life (oh how he would loathe his cultural obsolescence). Then with his face twisted in a mock grimace of effort, he'd tear the 1000-page tome in two and set down both halves with an exaggerated "whew." Later he'd tell me, "the trick is to start with just a few pages–then whatever you do, don't stop."

His other performance included an empty beer can, which in our family were also abundant in those days and infinitely more so than old phone books. John would set the Stroh's can on the floor and position one foot atop it, his face set in determination. Then he'd carefully rise to a one-footed stance, wobbling with tenuous balance. He'd linger for a moment like some overgrown Karate Kid, slightly bent at the hips and arms outstretched with his free foot floating behind him. Then, ever so slowly, he'd crouch down and tap the side of the can. The flimsy aluminum would instantaneously collapse. Johnny would triumphantly hold up the result of his effort – a perfect metal disc.

The conclusion of either feat would leave all of us laughing to the point of tears, no matter how many times we'd seen it.

John was also meticulous to a fault about everything. It started in childhood with the precise arrangement of toy soldiers. His books; beginning with Dr. Seuss, on to Edgar Rice Burroughs, and through to Faulkner and Don DeLillo; were always carefully ordered upon his shelves. Everything had to be just so. His wife of 13 years, Lisa (to whom Leaving Las Vegas is dedicated), was not allowed to touch anything on his writing desk. Procedures were subject to rigid John O'Brien flow charts. From the execution of laundry to the precise video recording of an episode of Twin Peaks or the Tracey Ullman Show (more obsolescence) – not one moment could be cropped, not even the opening credits despite being identical for each episode. Perhaps unsurprisingly, he also excelled in all branches of mathematics.

Johnny loved airplane food.

It was not the quality of the Salisbury steak or brownie that delighted him, but the geometric compartments in which they were served. Scrambled eggs were shaped in a cube, removing the distasteful concept of scrambled from the picture completely. Salad dressing and margarine, freed from sloppy communal bottles or tubs, came in neat little cups. And a moist towelette in a foil packet finished everything off.

The mini booze bottles must have been a bit more complex, but surely an important part of the proceedings. The first Wild Turkey came with the giddy excitement of air travel and its unique set of drinking rules. After all, this is when getting on an airplane, no matter how routine the reason, was synonymous with discovery and possibilities, long before it devolved into an experience mired in restriction and regulation (more obsolescence, but for John's sake I'll stop tagging it). A tittering stewardess would pluck the tiny bottle from the drinks tray for the good-looking flirtatious man in 23A. Drink number two would be much the same. Wild Turkey numbers three and four undoubtedly steered things into marginal territory. Embarrassment probably kicked in with number five or six when the stewardess's giggles were replaced with polite smiles (the guys in Tony's would call that a "tipping point"). After that, everyone knew the score and rote transactions undoubtedly ensued at regularly timed intervals until tray tables were in their upright and locked positions in preparation for landing, although "preparation" is a generous designation in this case.

I am not nearly as orderly as John was, but when I solidly pack an entire order of groceries into two reusable bags, John's ghost nods approvingly over my shoulder. After all, I've elevated a mundane task to a functioning three-dimensional game of Tetris. It is the same with math and numbers. Draw attention to any number in my life, and it magically transforms into a character. When I turned 54 earlier this year, it arrived by way of a simple equation: Twenty-one plus thirty-three. The twenty-one may be far far away regarding my years, but it's easy to love nonetheless: three times seven, could anything be more fitting than this blissful union of two prime numbers? More obviously twenty-one evokes Johnny's Las Vegas, with its dazzling cocktail waitresses delivering free booze to him on one side of the table and understanding blackjack dealers nodding and reassuring him on the other side. As for thirty-three, it would normally be a magical computation of three times eleven, with three being its bubbly self and eleven, yet another prime, reminding me that two parallel lines walk together forever and ever while never touching. But of course, thirty-three has indelibly transformed in my world. It's the age John was on the day he ended his life.

This is how people like John and me are wired. We are the result of math chromosome meets art chromosome. We both found our craft in writing. It is natural for our work to become equations of words driven by underlying theorems and corollaries.

Hence when, just a few paragraphs into Leaving Las Vegas, I read, "His point was made, and he moved along, in keeping with the tangential nature that must consume at least one of them. There is a bottle in his future--perhaps sooner a glass--elsewhere on the line. Sera is a circle, twenty-nine years around," I know there will be no games of chance in the subsequent pages of Leaving Las Vegas, that John has checked every option box for his characters right from the beginning. He has drawn the lines, and his characters will stay within them. Had John lived long enough for my revelation to bloom, he and I might have joked about it, How to diagram a novel in fifty easy words!

Since I so badly referenced that brief excerpt during the roundtable, I beg the reader to indulge me here. There is a woman (a circle) and a man (a straight line). The metaphor is perfect in its every permutation: in the primal symbols of female and male, and in the visual moment when Ben and Sera first glance off each other. Their tangential one-point contact is also an accurate representation of their relationship as a whole. His line does not bisect the circle or thread through its middle just as Ben does not penetrate Sera. After their brief and chaste affair, Sera will continue to roll around her diameter, and Ben's line will plod on. That line is resolute in its path and the liquor that marks it. Whether it comes to an end or continues along towards a spiritual vanishing point depends on how a person spends their Sunday morning. Sera's age, twenty-nine, is also a prime number, divisible only by itself and the number one.

And with that, I must pause to sigh.

Behold the clarity of the mathematical trappings behind John's work. My brother desired a world with straight edges and governing axioms. To that end, the lives of his characters obediently stayed in their designated compartments and followed Boolean laws. John's chapter titles alone demonstrate this: days dictate the action in Stripper Lessons and The Assault on Tony's, while cherries, bars, lemons, and plums beautifully delineate Leaving Las Vegas. Therein is the tragedy of John O'Brien; the one life he could not control was his own. But he died trying.

* * *

In all, there are more than 800 pages of John O'Brien including the four works explored in this volume: *Leaving Las Vegas* (Watermark Press, 1990), *The Assault on Tony's* (Grove 1996). *Stripper Lessons* (Grove 1997), and *Better*. (Akashic, 2009). All but *Leaving Las Vegas* were published posthumously, as was one short story "The Tic," which appeared in two anthologies, Las Vegas Noir and USA Noir (Akashic, 2008 and 2013, respectively). My brother did live to see one more of his works come to fruition, and in a place the reader is not likely to expect. It certainly took me by surprise.

It was about two decades ago. I was going about some mindless household chore while my three-year-old daughter watched The Rugrats. But when Tommy and Angelica started prattling on about a hidden cache of mysterious old toys, my head snapped. Familiarity washed over me. I sat down next to Jessie and blinked at the screen. The episode, "Toys in the Attic," had been written by John in 1992. He had sent me a copy of his draft because it was based on the two of us and toys that were in the attic of our childhood home. (Those playing along at home can file this note next to the one that assures, "Why yes indeed, James Bond creator Ian Fleming really did write the book *Chitty-Chitty-Bang-Bang*.")

When the show was over, I scurried to my file cabinet and unearthed John's original pages. He had told me he was unhappy with the final edits and therefore asked that the writing credit is listed under a pen name "Carroll Mine," which is the main character in John's novel *Stripper Lessons*.

"So I'll be able to prove I wrote the episode," John explained, "on the outside chance it wins some award or something." My brother's irritation over the Rugrats script felt completely moot now that he had captivated his tiny niece whom he never knew on account of being dead for more than five years. Thus a delicate tether was wrought, and even Miss Moneypenny blinked away one bittersweet tear.

The Assault on Tony's was first-draft quality, and there was nothing to be done about it. Had John lived to flesh out and polish Tony's, it might have been a great American novel, or maybe he would have shelved it. Left unfinished at the time of his death, I contributed an end to it I now loathe with a passion, although I've learned to forgive myself. That said, I am thankful for the rough edges in this book, which is a dangerous landscape dotted with emotional landmines for me that are also clues for solving the Rubik's cube of John O'Brien and his work.

For instance, there is Rudd's recollection of his job as a teenaged busboy: "Rudd was sixteen and bussing tables in a tony restaurant where even the dishwashers were Caucasian and the busboys were damn near transparent...everybody liked Rudd..." For me it is anything but an off-hand reference. In that scant excerpt, I see John subtly mimicking what he perceived to be our father's racism. Then I see a 33-year-old alcoholic writer remembering himself at 16 when he was sober and funny and working as a busboy at Tony's Restaurant at Kamm's Corners on Cleveland's near west side.

"There are these huge trays, Erin," John reported to me after his first night on the job. "And we have to fit everything from a table onto the tray - everything - then cover the whole mess with the table cloth and haul it on our shoulder into the kitchen."

And then this: "Fenton wasn't much of a man, his dad once told him during one of that man's many drunken binges," I want John to come back and reassure me that Dad never said this. I want him to quiet the voice inside me that knows this is a detail excised from John's vulnerable teen years.

The list of such references is entirely too long and painful for inclusion herein, but I cannot leave *Tony's* without mentioning the brief episode with "Cash and Cards," which commences on page 87 of the book. It left me with the troubling feeling that John himself might not be immune to all the racism in the novel. I invite readers to inspect the associated passages and decide for themselves. The mustard-kiss math, just two pages after the introduction of "Cash and Cards," almost makes up for the unfortunate passage. Almost.

Stripper Lessons, conversely, was a gift straight from heaven and my favorite piece of John's fiction. Carroll takes the stage and washes away all the booze and blood, making way for Johnny to come floating back. Those old parlor tricks may not be depicted amid the book's 201 pages, but that's the old Johnny winking at me from between the lines. I love the K'mon-n-Mart and that Carroll's stripper/angel is named Stevie (after Stevie Nicks, whom John thought was an unparalleled goddess). I love how an unruly epaulet upsets his whole world just as he garners the attention of a beautiful stripper: "He always assumed they were phony and didn't even unbutton, but fuck if one didn't unbutton itself, the goofy strap hanging sloppily off his shoulder, a nerd ID badge, like a pocket protector or a sign that says KICK ME."

Better, with its allusions to impossible genetic traps and a main character who shares the name William with our dad, left me with one haunting realization: John may have gotten as far away from his family as possible, but he could not escape his genetic mapping. Right or wrong, I honestly think that belief contributed more to his suicide than any other factor. John was convinced that he could never overcome the booze because it was part of his wiring. On the day that revelation bloomed, I lay flat on my back on the couch, tears streaming into my hair and ears as I imagined John morbidly joking about it: The calls, Mr. O'Brien, are coming from inside the house. John had been dead for 14 years.

As for "The Tik," Johnny shared the story with Mom, Dad and me more than thirty years ago.

May 13, 1988

Dear Mom and Dad,

Here's a story I wrote in January. It's a little atypical but it's my personal favorite. Since then I've been working on a novel. Please give this to Erin when you're done. See you soon.
Love,

John

"The Tik" swirls around a drug of the same name, a man stepping into his past, and a beautiful and treacherous woman named Melinda. Syringes, Wild Turkey, orgasms, splattering blood and blasé indifference round out this black, violent, and unapologetic offering. I don't know if it is a good story or a bad story, nor could I ever decide. All I see are the defense mechanisms of a young man standing naked before addiction. The short story John wrote so early in his writing career (the novel he references in the note is *Leaving Las Vegas*) also galvanizes what I believed for years. Although John mightily wielded the one weapon that might have saved him — the pen — in the end, it couldn't defend him from himself.

* * *

I had only read "The Tik," *Leaving Las Vegas,* and "Toys in the Attic" at the time of John's death. We unearthed his other novels from his Mac Color Classic, which packed a whopping 4MB memory and cost $1,400 in 1993 (sorry ... I promise that is the last of the obsolescence tags). The computer was shipped with his effects a few weeks after his death. The box also contained his wedding ring and his watch. The gun arrived months later. We sent the wedding ring to Lisa but the watch was more complicated.

On September 3, 1988, John purchased a "pre-owned" Rolex Oyster Perpetual Date from Slavick's Jewelers in Los Angeles. The watch had been professionally serviced and certified by Rolex and the numbered "official chronometer certification," sales receipt, original sales brochure, and paperwork for subsequent service work were all in the effects package along with the red Rolex seal that bears the famous crown. (And one more for the advanced class, John purchased his used Rolex for about $1,500. In the book, however, John describes Ben's timepiece as a "thirty-five-hundred-dollar Swiss watch," in case anyone was wondering where John placed himself on the food chain in relation to Ben.)

John's watch wasn't quite as upscale as the one the character Ben wore in the film version of Leaving Las Vegas, in which Nicolas Cage dons the pricier Daytona model, but it was his most prized possession. My brother loved his Rolex, as does Ben. To that end, John devotes two entire paragraphs (p. 120 – 122), to the description of Ben's parting with the watch, the proceeds of which he uses to purchase a few hours with "an overpriced hooker." This is how Sera is delivered unto him. Essentially, he relinquishes the one earthly object he values to secure an angel's guidance through his last days. That detail, one of the most significant yet subtle points in the book, is not noted in the film. I believe the omission would have infuriated my brother had he lived to see his characters glitter on the silver screen.

Dad wore the watch for a while. After he died in 2002, Mom gave it to me and I promptly deposited it atop that same file cabinet wherein the original "Toys in the Attic" script was housed. There it remained, however unceremoniously, until my daughter's 21st birthday.

"This is from your uncle," I told her and handed over the one object John cared so deeply about. It closed a loop of sorts. John had sent me his copy of Webster's Third New International Dictionary just two months before his death. The 2,662-page volume weighs 13 pounds and is stationed upon my writing desk.

As for the gun, Dad penned this brief note about it shortly after it arrived.

Although I've never inspected this gun – it is said to be owned by John S. O'Brien [per] Beverly Hills Police Dept. Detective Steve Miller. It was last fired on April 10, 1994.

I obtained it from BHPD in Sept. '94.

Bill O'Brien

Dad taped that on the unopened mailer, wrapped it all up, and stowed it away. At some point after his death, Mom gave the package to my husband Eric. It remained sealed until nearly 19 years after that final shot in 1994. I finally decided to open the box on January 4, 2013. I have no idea what happened that day; perhaps some cosmic switched toggled. Whatever the case, it was time.

The box felt at once too heavy and too light. I could not open it. I handed it to Eric as queasiness overwhelmed me. What if it was flecked with gore? I was shaky and flushed as he lifted the Smith and Wesson, a terrible handsome thing, from the box. The evidence tag was another story altogether. I had not expected that: official written verification of what Dad refused to acknowledge on the outside of this box. That rote slip of paper struck me at my core.

I took photos of the gun, wrapped it up, and gave it to my husband to slide back into its secret place. Go ahead and ask me if Leaving Las Vegas is autobiographical.

* * *

In his chilling yet comforting assertion, American neuroscientist and author David Eagleman tells us, "There are three deaths. The first is when the body ceases to function. The second is when the body is consigned to the grave. The third is that moment, sometime in the future, when your name is spoken for the last time."

With that I'd like to recognize the work and contributions of everyone who made this book possible, including Sara Dobie Bauer, Christie Danzey, Dorian D'Apice, Kelly Flamos, Carolyn Jack, Cassandra Jackson, Rob Jackson, Alok Khorana, Matt Marshall, Ben Mckelvey, Max McNeil, Dave Megenhardt, Melissa Nahra, Tanya Pilumeli, Anna Powaski, Rick Ridgeway, Patrick Snee, Bob Triozzi, Marina Vladova, and RA Washington.

Your words and commentary have extended my brother's longevity in a way only literature can. For that, I give you my most profound and solemn gratitude.

Erin

Appendix

The Tik
a short story

John O'Brien

Part of me wished that I had asked the cab to wait. I hadn't. I stared up at the big double doors, weathered from the desert sun, yes, but still so imposing that you half expected to see a muscled bodyguard when they opened. The doorbell didn't work. It never had. I felt the familiar quiver begin in the back of my neck as twice I dropped the ornate knocker, an upside-down black iron cross. I peered over my back to see if the cab was still in sight. The long drive was empty.

Despite the impending nightfall, I noticed the German shepherd asleep on the grass, his white face a beacon in the otherwise black lawn. I knew this dog and wondered if he would remember me. I walked over to nudge him awake.

When I had last left this house over ten years ago, I was certain that I was through with this all-consuming part of my life, but as I bent over to pet the dog, it was clear this place was far from finished with me; rather, like the dog, it was merely lying in wait for some new awakening. The shepherd lifted his head and growled, but whether the snarl was for me or something else, I did not know. I followed his gaze and was startled to find that I was being watched by the tall slim figure, standing where only moments before the closed doors had been.

"Timmers, you're back," she said, not at all surprised to see me.

I cringed at her easy, reflexive use of my nickname; at her prosaic manner of observation, as if I'd just returned from a short walk--when in fact I had been gone for a decade. This meeting was nothing less than heart stopping for me.

"Melinda, I ... I didn't hear the door open. You startled me," so much so, in fact, that I couldn't remember anything that I had planned to say. "You sound as if you've been expecting me." She ignored this.

"Come in," she said.

As I followed her through the foyer and into the heart of the house, I began to feel a sort of resignation; a feeling that, now that I had set things in motion, I could sit back and relax, free from the burden of decision making. It was not an unpleasant outlook.

"Christ," I said as we walked into the living room, it's windowed ceiling a full 20 feet above me. "I'd forgotten how damn big this place is."

"I doubt that," she responded. "Still drink bourbon?"

"Finally a question. Apparently there is at least one thing that you're not sure of." I was starting to feel cocky. How else could I feel? I'd come this far into the house, into my past. The less I thought about it, the better it felt. I was comfortable here. Melinda understood me in a way that no one else could.

"Not really, Timmers." She reached into an antique Spanish sideboard and extracted a dusty bottle of Wild Turkey.

"My brand, even. I'm impressed." I narrowed my eyes and grinned at her. Her presence was making me giddy. I was excited--this was so easy. She knew why I was here. It was like being in a cathouse--no pretense. You ask for sex and they give it to you. But a cathouse would seem like a church compared to this house.

"Your bottle, actually," she said.

"Fuck it," I said. "We can drink all we want later."

Without missing a beat she set down the bottle, picked up my hand, and turned silently toward the staircase. I willingly followed her determined walk and flowing silk robe. This was the beginning of the end of ten years anxiety. It seemed as if I'd barely been away. Right now nothing seemed less relevant than my time away from her.

But I did have that time, and I had to remember that. I had to remember the futile years of trying to ignore this hidden life, with Melinda and this extravagant house standing at the center. I had to remember why I was here.

Why was I here?

What if I did like it? Liking it--living it--had been the whole point. I was back now and it was time to unlearn compassion and let Melinda take me again.

We climbed the staircase to her bedroom; ten years since it had been our bedroom and yet it looked exactly the same to me. Perhaps it would always be our bedroom. Melinda dropped my hand and turned to face me. She stepped back and looked into my eyes as she untied her robe and let it fall to the floor. I was amazed at her perfection. Though life had left its many marks on my body, she was just as I remembered--flawless, still possessing all the curves and textures of a nineteen year old showgirl.

She unbuttoned my shirt and in a moment I, too, was naked. Melinda wrapped herself around me. I lifted her onto the bed, the raw heat rising inside of me. It was exactly as I remembered. I ran my hands along her thighs, stopping short of the cleft of her. Her nipples were hard and brown. I took one between my teeth, one between thumb and finger and bit and pinched with exacting pressure. Melinda cried out, but did not move to stop me. She was open beneath me, ready. It was time. I licked and tasted her until her legs quivered on the brink. I stopped short of her orgasm and lay on top of her breathing in the intermission. Finally, I pushed into her. She climaxed in waves, acute bursts of pleasure. I was close behind, teetering on that exquisite edge.

Melinda sensed this, as I knew she would, and stopped all her motion. At once my imminent climax was completely in her control. She slid from beneath me and sat up on the side of the bed. She opened the nightstand drawer. I waited, trembling, as she extracted a stainless steel tray and with slick efficiency prepared the injection. The glowing black fluid filled the syringe. My hardness raged. I swallowed against it all, my throat dry.

At that moment it was impossible for me to understand how I had stayed away from this drug--we called it "The Tik"--for all those years. I had never heard of it outside this room and had never looked for it elsewhere. Somehow I knew that it existed nowhere but here. This place was as much a part of The Tik as I, moments before, had been a part of Melinda. She lived here in a desert oasis with it, and the whole scene had always been one great, indivisible, seductive, eternal entity to me. I had once believed that I could escape it by running. Now I had run back, and was going to try to escape another way.

Melinda tapped the needle of the syringe with a long red fingernail. The sexual tension and my own anticipation had my heart nearly beating out of my chest. My bloodstream was primed to rush the drug to my brain. Melinda turned, ready with the needle. I closed my eyes and offered my arm.

The beautiful pinch.

As the hot fluid rushed through my veins, Melinda prepared another hypo and injected herself. Then she dropped the syringe onto the tray and kicked it as she lunged into me. As the stainless steel and empty vial clattered to the floor, Melinda clutched my waist and took me into her mouth. The heat of The Tik inside of me and the heat of Melinda's tongue outside of me combined into that perfect euphoria I'd known only within these walls. She held me on the brink for as long as she could. Then I yelled out, pumping into her.

The feeling of being alive poured over me, elemental and singular. We were finally together again.

The Tik.

We blinked in the aftermath, verifying it was real. I lay on my back, Melinda's head on my stomach. Then she reared up and playfully bit me. I laughed and pushed her off. Full of new energy, I bounded out of the bed and down the stairs, returning with the bottle of bourbon. Melinda already had her panties on and was rolling up her fishnets. I sucked the bottle as I watched her dress. She grabbed it from me and took a big swallow.

"I have a surprise for you," she said. She shoved the bottle back into my hand and pulled open the door of what had been my closet. I was stunned. Before me hung all my old clothes, just as I had left them.

I laughed. "Unfuckingbelievable. Do you still have the Jag, too?"

"In the garage," she said.

Nothing had changed.

Melinda and the drug were working in perfect harmony. My head spun with satisfaction and lust. I grinned wildly and shook on the leather jacket that had always fit me like a second skin. It still did. My boots, my jeans, everything was in place. I gulped some more bourbon and pounced on Melinda. We fell onto the bed and I ripped off the black lace bra she had just put on. She laughed as the zipper on my jacket scratched her. We fucked again, more perfunctorily this time, then got dressed.

After finishing the bottle of bourbon we went down to the garage. Melinda's vintage Jag, a black 1967 XKE, was still in perfect shape, just as I, by now, expected everything to be. The car had also fit me. I slid into the driver's seat and palmed the bulb of the stick shift. Melinda's perfume blended with the smell of leather and night air. We squealed down the driveway and onto the moneyed sidestreet. The rag top was down and the wind blew Melinda's hair all around. I flew through a red light. We vanished into the night.

We headed for the strip, battling traffic. I didn't mind. I basked in the stares this beautiful woman and car garnered beneath the streetlights and neon.

"Let's go to the Barbary Coast," I said.

"The Barbary Coast? You've got to be kidding," said Melinda."Why?"

"Dunno," I said, shrugging my shoulders, "The $3.99 prime rib dinner?"

Melinda laughed, throwing her head back. "Oh Timmers," she said, "I'd forgotten how you make me laugh."

We parked off the strip and starting walking hand and hand through the crowd. The Tik pulsed through me and mixed with the bourbon. Melinda was on my arm. I was ten feet tall.

Overweight Midwesterners stared at the two of us, wishing they could be us. We were the Las Vegas they came to see. A middle-aged man in Bermuda shorts eyed Melinda's long legs.

"Loosest slots on the strip," I said to him with a conspiratorial nod as we passed. Completely stunned, he looked up at me, his mouth agape. Melinda and I folded with laughter, then broke into a run.

After a few minutes, Melinda stopped, breathless, and turned to me. She squeezed my hand. Her nails broke the skin.

"It feels so good to have you back, Tim," she said.

I pushed her against the cold brick wall and put my mouth on hers while pressing my thigh between her legs.

"I love you," I whispered. My hand was sticky with blood.

She returned my kiss, our tongues rolling together until Melinda pulled back.

"Why then," she said, "are you going to make me go in there?" She nodded toward the billowing entrance of the Coast.

"Come on," I said. "I feel so good. I feel like slumming. And if we don't find any action in there," I, indicated the space in front of me with a grandiose sweep of my arm, "The entire strip awaits us." We stepped through the forced air plenum and into the clanging miasma of the casino.

A semi-attractive blond with a very large chest caught my attention. She was sitting alone at a black jack table.

"I'm going to the girls' room," Melinda shouted over the cacophony of bells and chimes that rang from the slot carousels. "I'll catch up to you in a couple of minutes."

I nodded and watched her meander off as did most of the people she passed. The fishnet stockings had that effect.

I sat down next to the blond and threw $100 on the table. The dealer set a short stack of chips in front of me as a cocktail waitress in a bad pirate costume appeared at my elbow.

"A double bullshot," I said, placing a chip on her tray.

"What's that?" said the blond as she slurped at a frothy blender drink.

"It's beef bouillon and vodka," I said, peering at my cards.

She wrinkled her nose into a grimace. "Ewww! Why are you drinking that?" The end of her straw was coated in waxy orange lipstick.

"I'm hungry." I said. After all, I was. I nodded yes to a hit from the dealer.

"That's so gross," she said.

"Fuck you," I said. Maybe semi-attractive was too generous a description for her, stacked or not. The bad casino lighting wasn't shoring up her odds either. "Now shut up and finish your snow cone."

"Okay, I will," she said. "And then you can."

"I can what?" I said, rolling my eyes. The waitress set down my drink with exactly the speed a pre-tip buys. I placed another chip on her tray and turned back to the blond.

"You can fuck me," she said as the dealer flipped over his Jack and ace.

"Who the fuck are you?" With characteristically perfect timing and an equally perfect brunette, led by the hand, Melinda intervened. The blond sized up the two women and picked up her drink. "I'm more than you could handle anyway," she said, then collected her remaining chips and walked away, flipping us off.

"Tim, this is Teena," said Melinda, not even looking after the blond. "She's new in town. Just got a job as a waitress over at the Peppermill."

"After I finish the training course," said Teena. "Of course," she added, giggling at her own quip.

"Right," said Melinda. "After you finish the training course." She wrapped an arm around Teena's waist and turned to me. "She's coming home with us for a nightcap." One look at Teena and I could see that Melinda had bribed her with the coke she always kept in her purse.

"Hi, Tim. I saw you walk in and thought you were really cute. I'm really glad to meet you," said Teena. She seemed like a willing little lamb, naïve and very sexy. Exactly what I'd had in mind.

"With that perky attitude," I said through a toothy grin, "my bet is you'll sail right through that training course." Teena gave me a prom queen smile. Perfect, just like everything else so far.

"So what do you say, Tim?" asked Melinda, though she already knew the answer. "Nightcaps at our place?"

Our place.

"That sounds just fine," I said. "First let's have a drink for the road." I pushed a chip towards the dealer and steered the girls around to the bar. "Will you be riding with us, Teena, or do you have your own car?"

"Teena will follow us out to the house," said Melinda, lifting an eyebrow down the bar.

I smiled at Teena.

"What can I get for you?" said the bartender, one eye eclipsed by a fake black eyepatch.

Melinda looked at me. "Make a wish," she said.

I motioned Teena to park next to the Jag in the garage. Melinda took Teena inside to show her around while I looked over Teena's Honda and then locked up. I went in the back door of the house and found Melinda and Teena necking in the kitchen. I didn't seem to disturb them.

"Save some for me, Mel," I said. "Anyone want a drink?"

"Tequila," said Melinda.

"Got any champagne?" asked Teena.

I headed for the sideboard to crack open a new bottle of bourbon.

"Join us upstairs when you're ready, Timmers," Melinda shouted down the hall. She was anxious despite her cool veneer. It had been a long time for her too. I also was eager to do a number on Teena, but something vague seemed to be holding me back. Fuck that, I thought, and took the longest drink of bourbon in my life.

By the time I got up to the bedroom, Melinda's face was buried between Tina's legs. Teena seemed a little dazed but was holding up her end quite well, no doubt aided by the small mountain of coke next to her on the nightstand. Melinda saw me and bolted upright. She was covered with sweat.

"Fuck her, Tim," she said. "Fuck her proper."

Teena rolled over and did another line, then she lay back on the bed.

"Yeah, fuck me," she said.

I did. I was rough but she took it. When I got off her bruises starting to form on the insides of her thighs. I reached for the bourbon and watched her and Melinda work on each other. I felt strange. The Tik still moved through me, though now at a even keel. I drank more bourbon.

I drank for a long time.

Melinda screamed and dug her nails into Teena's skin. Teena threw her head back on the pillow. Melinda rolled over and beckoned me. My head was spinning. I placed a hand on either of Teena's knees and opened her as Melinda reached for the nightstand. I centered all my consciousness on Teena. I focused my whole body on my mouth, and my mouth on her. Melinda moved on the bed. I heard a whisper of rushing air. Teena stiffened and bucked under me. A hot spray rained across my back. Something clinked against the wall. I squeezed Teena's waist with all my strength. Tears came to my eyes. Teena's body went limp.

I lay hugging her, my breath so fast. The room was quiet. After a time I looked up at Melinda. She smiled and wiped the blood from her eyes. She got off the bed and picked up the straight razor, which she had thrown against the wall. She dropped it in the nightstand drawer.

"You okay, Timmers?" she asked. "I know it's been a while." She paused, then reached back into the drawer. "Maybe it's time for another shot."

"No," I said. "Not yet."

I picked up the bourbon and had a sip. Melinda closed the drawer and turned towards the bathroom.

"Suit yourself, but we shouldn't wait too long," she said. "I'm going to clean up. Will you take care of that?"
She nodded at the blood soaked bed and the still body, naked and staring wide-eyed at the ceiling.

"Of course I will," I said. "Don't I always?"

I finished the bourbon as Melinda closed the bathroom door behind her. Out the window, dawn announced itself quietly with a barely perceptible change of color in the east. A car started off in the distance and I reflexively glanced at the garage door. It was still locked. I really didn't worry. Melinda and I had always led a charmed existence. I sighed and put on my pants.

"Wash my back, Tim," Melinda called from the shower when she heard me enter the bathroom. I opened the curtain and soaped up my hands. I massaged her back as I washed it.

"Ahhh, that feels good," she said. "Get in here. I'm ready for a good fucking."

She put her cheek against the wall and closed her eyes. I pulled her razor from my back pocket. With one motion I grabbed her hair and drew the blade across her throat. For an instant she stretched her neck out, exposing it even more, and then she slumped quietly to the bottom of the tub. I turned off the water and went into the bedroom, dropped the razor into her nightstand.

I cleaned up and finished dressing in the clothes that I had arrived in the day before. I kissed Teena's forehead. I kissed Melinda's hand and held it to my mouth for a long time. Downstairs I lit a small fire on the love seat in the living room, then went to the kitchen and turned on all the gas jets. On my way out to the garage I stopped and, as an afterthought, picked up my leather jacket.

I backed the Jag out of the drive and looked for but did not see the German shepherd. It suddenly occurred to me how very old he must have been. As I put the Jag into gear, my eyes paused at the mailbox, an unlikely witness. I pulled away and, driving down the road, watched it disappear in the rear view mirror. I thought about how badly I needed to sleep.

www.ingramcontent.com/pod-product-compliance
Lightning Source LLC
Chambersburg PA
CBHW022005090426
42741CB00007B/902